Painting Your Favorite Flowers

STEP BY STEP

Mary M. Wiseman

NORTH LIGHT BOOKS

CINCINNATI, OHIO

www.nlbooks.com

Dedication

To my husband, Roy, and our three children, Stacey, Matthew and Sarah, who have loved, encouraged and believed in me always. Thank you for giving me roots and wings.

For all the students who have touched my life and forever made it better. I sometimes wonder who is the teacher and who is the student.

To all those who have been on my path in the past, and those in the future who will encourage and challenge me to keep teaching and learning forever.

Acknowledgments

I would like to recognize and thank Kathy Kipp for taking a class from me at the Heart of Ohio Tole convention. Her belief in my strength to teach a rose evolved into a book. Thanks to the patience and guidance of Jennifer Long, this book has become a reality.

Thank you to Christine Polomsky for making the color photography of the leaf and rose just what I had envisioned, and for being the student while she snapped the photos.

My thanks to the paint manufacturers and suppliers of the products that helped create the projects in this book.

Finally, thank you to all the students who over the years have encouraged me to paint flowers.

Painting Your Favorite Flowers Step by Step. Copyright © 2001 by Mary M. Wiseman. Manufactured in China. All rights reserved. The patterns and drawings in this book are for the personal use of the decorative painter. By permission of the author and publisher, they may be either hand-traced or photocopied to make single copies, but under no circumstances may they be resold or republished. It is permissible for the purchaser to paint the designs contained herein and sell them at fairs, bazaars and craft shows. No other part of this book may be reproduced in any form or by any electronic or mechanical means including information storage and retrieval systems without permission in writing from the publisher, except by a reviewer, who may quote brief passages in a review. Published by North Light Books, an imprint of F&W Publications, Inc., 1507 Dana Avenue, Cincinnati, Ohio 45207. (800) 289-0963. First edition.

Other fine North Light Books are available from your local bookstore, art supply store or direct from the publisher.

05 04 03 02 01   5 4 3 2 1

Library of Congress Cataloging-in-Publication Data
Wiseman, Mary M.
   Painting your favorite flowers step by step / Mary M. Wiseman.--1st ed.
     p. cm.
  Includes index.
  ISBN 1-58180-024-X (pbk : alk. paper)
   1. Acrylic painting--Technique. 2. Flowers in art. 3. Decoration and ornament--Plant
forms. I. Title.
TT385 .W57 2001
745.7'23--dc21   00-062844

Editor: Jennifer Long
Production Coordinator: Emily Gross
Designer: Lisa Buchanan
Materials and step-by-step photography: Christine Polomsky
Finished artwork photography: Al Parrish

About the Author

Mary M. Wiseman has been painting since 1974. Just married and looking to start a new hobby, she went to her local craft shop and was encouraged to take a tole painting class. Oil paints were the medium of choice at the time. After completing a class on wild roses taught by Mary Jo Leisure, she knew her passion for painting had begun.

Mary continued to study many styles of decorative painting and became a member of the Society of Decorative Painters (SDP) in 1977. Joining her local chapter, the Great Lakes Decorative Painters, she was able to study the styles of many artists in the decorative art field.

In 1980, Mary was encouraged by her local instructor, Mary Luckstead, to teach a class through adult education. The mother of three small children under the age of five, she began her career as a teacher. As a stay-at-home mom, she went from teaching a class in adult education to setting up a home studio, where she has instructed classes for twenty years.

In 1985, a new craft shop opened in her area and Mary was able to expand her love of teaching art to designing. She formed a partnership with Mary Ann King, a basket weaver. Together they formed Marys Publications; Mary Ann created baskets on which Mary painted. They published two books—Yours, Mine and Ours volumes one and two—along with over thirty pattern packets. They also team-taught and chaired basket conventions in Michigan for over twelve years. During this time, Mary began to paint in acrylics and design other art pieces for publication and instruction.

Mary has instructed at the Heart of Ohio Tole convention since 1986 and has taught at the last fourteen SDP conventions. She has traveled to share her artwork with chapters and shops throughout the United States and Canada for the last twelve years.

In 1998–99, Mary was selected as a developing skills artist for the Decorative Painter (the magazine published by SDP), where she created three designs that shared her love of flowers, fruit and scenery. Over the years of learning, teaching and designing, Mary has created hundreds of designs on wood, canvas, metal and fabric. She has been featured in Decorative Artist's Workbook and other magazines. Her design "Bowl of Fruit on a Bread Box" was published in the book The Best of Decorative Painting (North Light Books). Mary enjoys painting many styles of art, but her passion still remains in creating realistic floral and fruit compositions.

Mary's true love, teaching, has been her motivation in the decorative arts. It is her belief that anyone can enjoy creating a beautiful piece of art when taught good art skills and principles, combined with practice. Mary continues to learn, teach, design and promote decorative painting. She is presently the vice-president/president-elect of the Society of Decorative Painters.

She invites you to expand your talents and meet new friends by joining the Society of Decorative Painters.

Society of Decorative Painters
393 N. McLean Blvd.
Wichita, KS 67203-5968
Phone (316) 269-9300
Fax (316) 269-9191
E-mail sdp@southwind.net

Write to Mary at:
12856 Whitfield
Sterling Heights, MI 48312

Table of Contents

Introduction

Over the last twenty-two years of teaching decorative painting, many of my students have expressed a desire to paint soft, pretty flowers. My hope in creating *Painting Your Favorite Flowers Step by Step* is to help this desire become a reality.

Many acrylic painters want to achieve a more realistic look in their flower painting. It is my goal to teach you, through each project in this book, how to achieve this look by practicing brush control, learning the relationship between the background and the design, and controlling values and intensity. Each design is painted from the first step to the last with a very achievable method of building value changes.

The choice of surfaces will provide you the opportunity to work on wood, metal and china. You will also learn how to make the backgrounds interesting using new background treatments that will enhance the design.

It is my goal to help you increase your painting skills with each project, while educating you on art principles that will have a positive effect on all your creative endeavors in the future.

Thank you for allowing me to share my techniques with you.

Materials

Paints

All the projects in this book are painted in acrylics. I used the following brands: Golden Acrylics, DecoArt Heavenly Hues, DecoArt Americana, Delta Ceramcoat and Plaid FolkArt. You may choose to use a color conversion chart to convert my colors to your favorite brand.

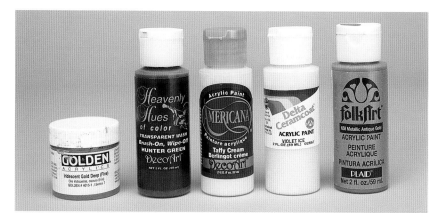

Brushes

The brushes and supplies listed below and on page 7 are what I prefer; however, you may substitute your favorite brands.

- A. 1-inch (25mm) polyfoam brush
- B. thin blade, bent handle palette knife for mixing
- C. Royal Majestic series 4700, 1-inch (25mm) wash brush
- D. Winsor & Newton Regency Gold series 560, 1-inch (25mm), ¾-inch (19mm), ½-inch (12mm), ¼-inch (6mm) and ⅛-inch (3mm); Loew-Cornell series 7400, ⅜-inch (10mm) and ⅝-inch (15mm) angles
- E. Loew-Cornell Maxine's Mop series 220, ½-inch (12mm)
- F. Loew-Cornell no. 6 fabric round brush
- G. Winsor & Newton Regency Gold series 550, no. 2, no. 4 and no. 6 filberts
- H. Bette Byrd Miracle Blender series 450, no. 6
- I. Winsor & Newton Regency Gold series 520, no. 1, no. 2, no. 4 and no. 6 rounds
- J. Loew-Cornell series 7050, 10/0 script liner
- (Not shown) Langnickel series 5005, no. 6 round; 1-inch (25mm) rake; no. 6 flat

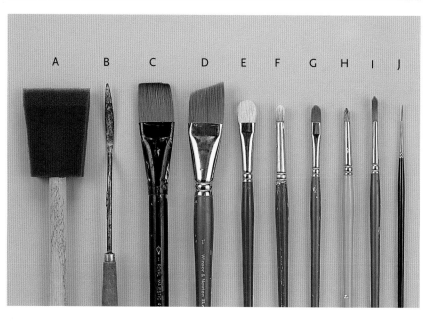

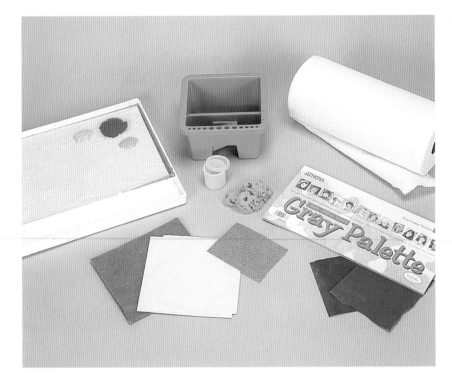

Painting Supplies

- tracing paper
- stylus
- fine-point pen
- black, gray and white transfer paper
- Masterson Sta-Wet palette
- 1-ounce (30ml) paint pots/containers
  with lids for storing mixes (if not using a
  wet palette)
- disposable waxed palette paper
- brush basin
- paper towels
- 320-grit wet/dry sandpaper
- tack rag
- sea sponge
- soft rags and scraps of T-shirt material

Sealers and Finishing Products

- Designs From the Heart Wood Sealer
- J.W. etc. White Lightning
- Krylon Matte Finish spray, no. 1311
- Americana Acrylic Sealer/ Finisher
  DAS13, matte
- J.W. etc. Right-Step Matte Varnish

Techniques

Transferring a Pattern

1 Lay tracing paper over the pattern. Use a fine-point pen to trace the main pattern lines.

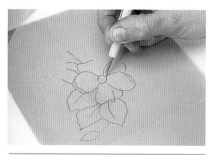

2 Position the tracing on the surface. Slide a piece of transfer paper underneath. Using a stylus, trace over the design lines.

3 Lift the pattern to see that the lines are transferring.

Chisel Edge

This refers to the edge of the brush where all the bristles end.

Palette Mixing

dark

light

Use a palette knife to mix two or more colors together on the palette.

Brush Mixing

1 Pick up the first color.

2 Pick up the second color.

3 Blend the two colors together on a clean area of the palette, walking the brush until the two colors blend to make another color.

Fully Loading Your Brush

1 Blot most of the water out of the bristles onto a paper towel.

2 Pull the color from the paint pile and blend one side of the brush. The brush should be held at a 45° angle; this is blending position. The color should blend up to, but not into, the ferrule of the brush.

3 Flip the brush over and blend the other side.

Dressing the Brush

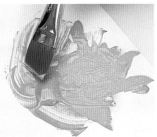

1 On a damp brush, pick up a touch of paint of a thinner consistency than used in loading the brush.

2 Blend the color into all the hairs of the brush, flipping the brush over to blend paint into both sides. This may be referred to as a "dirty brush" or "dirty wash." You can now load a stronger color onto the brush.

Washes

1 Load thin color into the brush.

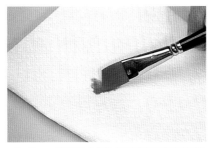

2 Blot the brush lightly on a paper towel.

3 Stroke the color over the area.

Basecoating (Blocking In)

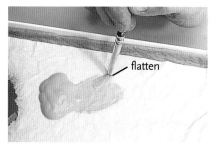

1 **Angle Brush**
Fully load the brush. Pull paint from the pile and completely blend the color through all the brush hairs.

2 Using shape-following strokes, block in the area.

3 **Round Brush**
Pull from the pile of paint. Flatten the brush hairs and blend the color through the hairs.

Side Loading

4 Press the brush down in larger areas and pull up on the hairs as you pull the brush into tighter areas.

1 Blot and pinch out all the water in the brush.

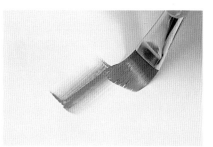

2 Corner load (dip only one corner of the brush bristles) into the desired color.

3 Blend one side of the brush. Allow the color to fade across the width of the brush, fading to nothing.

4 Flip the brush over and blend the other side. Straddle the line to create a soft edge of color.

Side-Load Float

  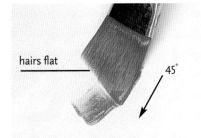

1 Lay the angle brush on a paper towel to blot the excess water out.

2 Dip the corner of the brush into the color.

3 Lay the brush onto the palette and pull the brush to allow the color to blend over toward the short side of the brush.

Back-to-Back Float

4 Flip and blend the other side of the brush.

5 Float the color in the desired area. The color should graduate from strong color to no color (value out).

1 Dip the long edge of the angle brush into the paint.

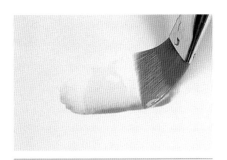  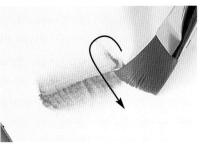

2 Blend on the palette.

3 Float one side of the brush.

4 Flip the brush over and float the other side of the brush. Straddle the line, blending over it.

Side-Load Wash

1 Thin the color with water to an ink-like consistency using a palette knife.

2 Blot water out of the brush.

3 Corner load the brush, then blend the color through the brush.

4 Wash the color onto the desired area.

Building Shading

1 Side load the brush with the shade value. Float the color, starting the brush at the widest area. Lay the brush flat and pull toward the narrow area, releasing the hairs from the surface as the area gets tighter. The color should value out about two-thirds of the way across the area.

2 Using a small brush, side-load float a darker value in all the shade areas to deepen the color.

Building Highlighting

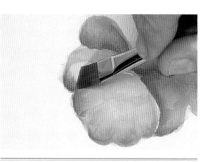

3 Side-load float the darkest value to reinforce the triangular areas and deepest shades.

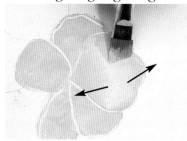

1 Side-load float a light value. Increase the amount of color and decrease the amount of water. Start the color in the largest area. Use a back-to-back float to apply color to areas such as this petal.

2 Repeat the previous color or use a value lighter than the last color applied. Using a smaller brush, float the color on top of and within the last color.

Drybrushing

1 Using a Betty Byrd no. 6 Miracle Blender, tip into the paint.

2 Press the bristles down onto the palette and apply pressure as the color is blended into the brush hairs.

3 Apply the color to the desired area, pressing hard on the hairs where more color is desired and releasing the pressure where less color is desired. Move the brush in a circular motion while holding it at a 45° angle.

Eliminating Harsh Lines

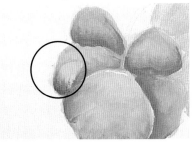

1 A harsh line appears when two colors are next to each other and need a transitional color to achieve a value transition.

2 With water, thin some of the base color or a value of color between the two colors. Side load the color onto a damp brush.

Mopping

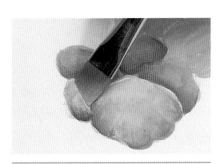

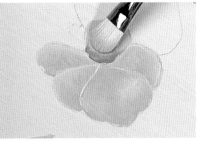

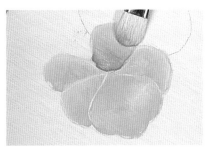

3 Place the brush down and allow the color to go over the area to soften the line.

1 While the color is still wet, lightly pat over it to soften.

2 The color softened.

Pat-Pull Color (Walking the Brush)

1 Blot most of the water from the brush.

2 Side load the brush.

3 Set the brush down as if to float the color. Pull the brush and then back the brush up.

4 Pull and back up again.

Patting in Color (Pity-Pat)

5 Pull and back up again.

1 Load as for the pat-pull. Lay the brush down in the desired area.

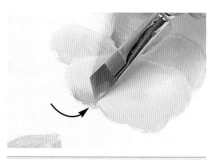

2 Pat the color down.

Skizzling

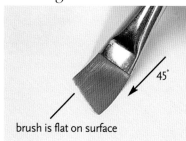

brush is flat on surface

45°

1 Corner load and side-load float. Lay the brush flat. Begin to zigzag one direction.

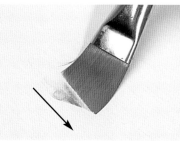

2 Zigzag in the opposite direction.

3 Now back to the first side.

4 Back to the opposite side again. Always keep the brush flat.

5 This creates a back-and-forth pattern.

Tapping In

1 Fully load a round brush and tap in the first color.

2 Finishing the first color.

3 While the first color is still wet, tap in the second color.

Comma Stroke

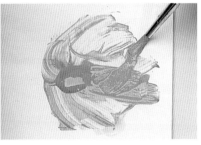

1 Fully load the round brush with color. Roll the hairs as the brush is pulled from the paint.

press

2 Press the hairs down with full pressure. Hold the brush perpendicular to the surface. It is helpful to use your other hand as a brace to steady the hand executing the stroke.

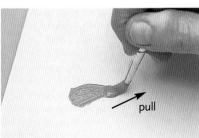

pull

3 Begin to pull the hairs of the brush. While pulling, begin to lift the brush and decrease the pressure on the brush hairs.

release

4 Release the brush hairs and ride the point of the round brush.

Liner Brush Dots

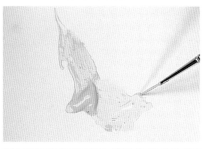

1 Fully load the brush. Don't thin the paint with water.

2 With the brush perpendicular to the surface, press the tip down to make a dot. The dots will vary according to how much pressure you apply to the tip.

Press Dots

1 Fully load a liner brush or a no. 2 round. With the brush perpendicular to the surface, press down.

2 Pick the brush up.

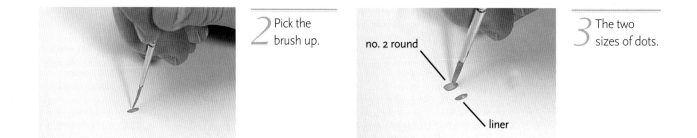

no. 2 round

liner

3 The two sizes of dots.

Pulling With a Liner

1 Fully load the liner brush with thin color.

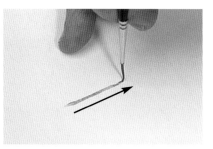

straight

2 Keeping the brush straight up on the very tip of the liner, start to pull toward your body.

3 Keep steady pressure until the line is finished.

Spattering

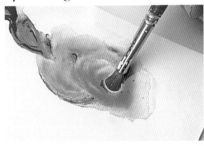

1 Thin the paint to an ink-like consistency and load a no. 6 round fabric brush.

2 Blot lightly on a paper towel.

3 Holding the brush, pull back on the hairs with your thumb, then let the hairs go. The closer you hold the brush to the surface, the heavier the spattering will be.

Sponging

1 Dampen the area to be sponged with water.

2 Wet the sponge with water, squeeze out the excess and touch the sponge into color. Press the sponge into the area you dampened.

3 Keep pressing the sponge onto the area, turning in different directions.

Stenciling

1 Load a Langnickel no. 6 round brush with paint. Pounce the excess paint out of the brush. Pounce straight up and down into the stencil opening.

2 Remove the stencil. You can clean up any stray marks with a damp Q-tip while the paint is still wet.

Painting Leaves

Cylinder Shaped – Floated Light Values

1 Base in solidly with Jade Green.

2 Apply the first light value with a side-load float of Reindeer Moss Green.

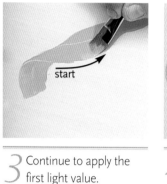

3 Continue to apply the first light value.

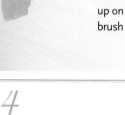

4

5

6

7 Apply the first light value over all of the light areas on the other side of the leaf.

8 Apply the second light value with a mix of Reindeer Moss Green + Titanium White. Apply this color within the areas you painted before.

9 Side-load float the first shade with Light Avocado + Jade Green.

10 Continue the first shade.

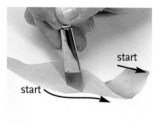

11

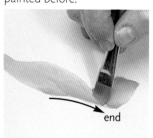

12

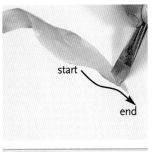

13 Shade the tip.

14 This shows the first shading completed.

15 Apply a vein line to the leaf using a liner brush and the mix from step 8 thinned with water.

16 Deepen the shade in the triangular areas with Light Avocado + Midnite Green.

17 Continue to deepen the darks.

18

19 Wash over the entire leaf to unify it using Light Avocado.

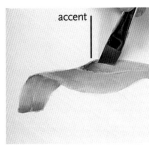

20 Side-load float an accent color of Cranberry Wine.

21

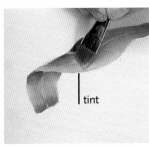

22 Side-load float a tint of Mauve + French Mauve.

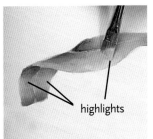

23 Apply a final high-light to the light areas using TitaniumWhite + Reindeer Moss Green.

24 The finished leaf.

Cube Shaped – Drybrushed Light Values

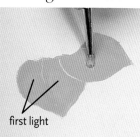

first light

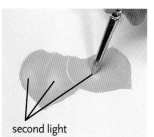

second light

1 Base in with Jade Green.

2 Drybrush the first light value with Reindeer Moss Green.

3 Continue the first light value.

4 Lighten Reindeer Moss Green with Titanium White and drybrush a second light value, applying less pressure on the brush.

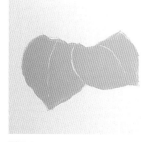

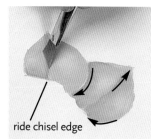
ride chisel edge

5 Apply the first shade using a side-load float of Light Avocado + Jade Green.

6 Continue the shading.

7

8 First shade complete.

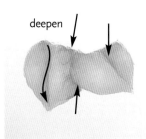
deepen

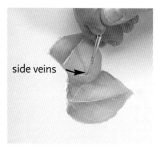
side veins

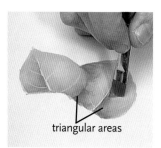
triangular areas

9 Reinforce the shade areas with Light Avocado, staying inside the previous application.

10 Add the vein lines with the mix from step 4, adding more Titanium White.

11 Continue the vein lines.

12 Deepen the triangular areas with Light Avocado + Black Green.

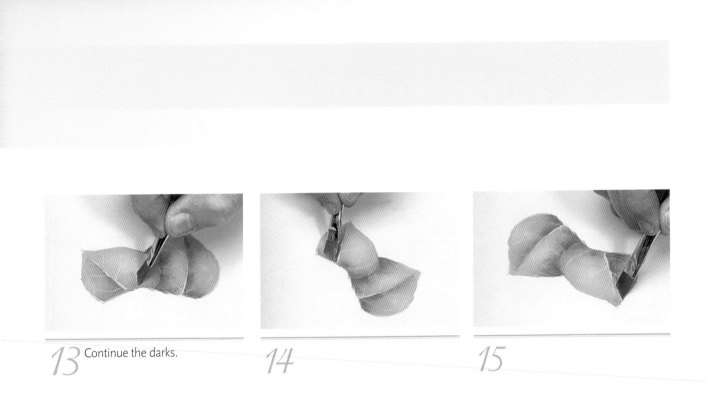

13 Continue the darks.

14

15

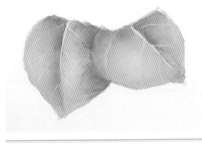

16 The darks completed.

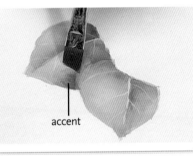

accent

17 Using a float of Cranberry Wine, add the accent color.

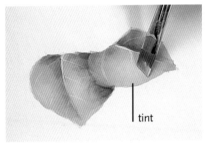

tint

18 Brush mix Mauve + French Mauve for a tint.

19 Wash over the leaves with thinned Light Avocado to unify the blending.

20 Drybrush final highlights in the center of the light areas. Reinforce the vein lines by adding more Titanium White to the light mix.

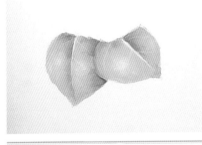

21 The leaves are finished.

Wild Roses

on a Towel Holder

Wild roses are a lovely, graceful flower. The very first flower I painted was a wild rose, so it seemed like a good place to begin our projects. These roses are painted on a towel holder that will grace your bathroom or kitchen. In this lesson you will learn to **paint petals that have flips and turns,** creating depth and value change.

Color Mixes

Mix 1
2 parts Antique Rose +
1 part Cool Neutral

Mix 2
2 parts Mix 1 + 1 part
Buttermilk

Mix 3
1 part Mix 2 + 1 part
Buttermilk

Mix 4
2 parts Buttermilk +
1 part Mix 3

Mix 5
1 part Jade Green +
1 part Taffy Cream

Mix 6
1 part Mix 5 + 1 part
Buttermilk

Mix 7
2 parts Midnite Green +
1 part Jade Green

Mix 8
1 part Mix 9 + 1 part
Light Buttermilk

Mix 9
1 part Mix 8 + 1 part
Taffy Cream

Mix 10
1 part Midnite Green + 2
parts Taffy Cream

This pattern may be hand-traced or photocopied for personal use only. Enlarge at 200% on a photocopier to return to full size.

Materials

Surface
- This 14" × 5" (35.6cm × 12.7cm) wooden towel holder is available from Viking Woodcrafts, Inc., 1317 8th St. SE, Waseca, MN 56093. Phone: (800) 361-0115. Fax: (507) 835-3895. Web site: www.vikingwoodcrafts.com.

DecoArt Americana Acrylic Paints
- Antique Rose DA156
- Blue Mist DA178
- Buttermilk DA3
- Cadmium Yellow DA10
- Cool Neutral DA89
- Jade Green DA57
- Light Avocado DA106
- Light Buttermilk DA164
- Midnite Green DA84
- Taffy Cream DA5

Golden Acrylics
- Iridescent Gold

Brushes
- ¼-inch (6mm), ⅜-inch (10mm), ½-inch (12mm) and ⅝-inch (15mm) angle brushes
- 10/0 script liner
- polyfoam brush
- 1-inch (25mm) wash brush

Additional Supplies
- tracing paper
- gray transfer paper
- 320-grit wet/dry sandpaper
- tack rag
- wet palette or paint pots
- J.W. etc. White Lightning
- J.W. etc. Right-Step Matte Varnish

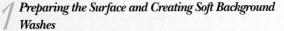

leaf A

1 Preparing the Surface and Creating Soft Background Washes

Unassembling the towel rack will make it easier to paint, so first remove the side towel brackets. Using a polyfoam brush, apply one coat of J.W. etc. White Lightning to the front, back, sides and towel bar. After this coat is dry, sand, then use a tack rag to wipe off the dust. Using a 1-inch (25mm) wash brush, apply three washes of Light Buttermilk thinned with water, allowing each coat to dry before applying the next. When dry, sand lightly with sandpaper and wipe off the dust with a tack rag. Transfer the pattern with gray transfer paper. When transferring the pattern, only the main lines of the objects are needed; it's best to transfer flower flips, leaf veins and vines after the first colors are applied. Mix the colors as instructed on page 23 and store on a wet palette or in small paint pots. Make enough of each mixture to last through the entire project—you'll need at least a quarter-sized puddle of each mix. Wet the background behind the design with clean water. Let the water settle into the wood just until the sheen of the water disappears; the surface should still be cool to the touch. Thin the following colors to a wash consistency and side load them on a ⅝-inch (15mm) angle brush. Pat them into the background in the appropriate area, working one section at a time until you've completed the background. Start with Cool Neutral. Apply all the way around the design, keeping the color deeper close to the design and fading out as far as the design elements extend. If a harsh line develops, stroke over it immediately with a clean, damp brush. When dry, wet the areas again and pat Mix 2 into some of the triangular areas. Repeat in some of the other triangular areas with Blue Mist and Mix 8. With Mix 10, wash in the leaf marked A. Side-load float Mix 8 at the base of the leaf to deepen the shading.

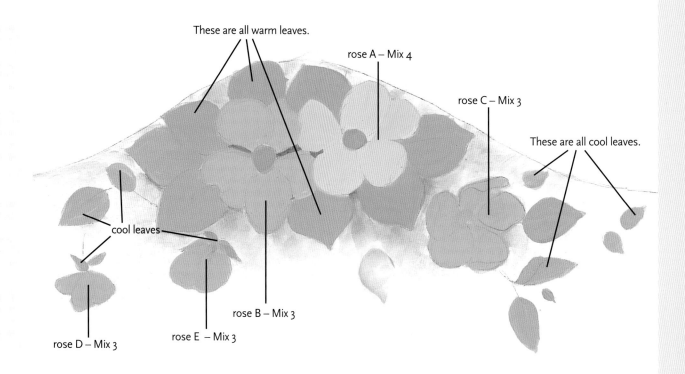

These are all warm leaves.

rose A – Mix 4

rose C – Mix 3

These are all cool leaves.

cool leaves

rose D – Mix 3

rose E – Mix 3

rose B – Mix 3

2 *Basecoating the Flowers and Leaves*

Block in the flowers and leaves with a fully loaded ⅜-inch (10mm) angle brush, using the colors listed below. Each object may require more then one coat to achieve opaque coverage—allow the paint to dry between coats.

- *Block in the warm leaves and flower centers with Mix 5.*
- *Block in rose A with Mix 4.*
- *Block in roses B, C, D and E with Mix 3.*
- *Block in the cool green leaves and calyx with Mix 9.*

Transfer the remaining pattern detail lines before proceeding to the next step.

3 Applying Shading to the Flowers and Light Values to the Leaves

Side load a ½-inch (12mm) or ⅜-inch (10mm) angle brush with Mix 3. Side-load float a light shading on all the roses. Sometimes it's helpful to dampen the surface with water before applying the color. The color should value out (graduate from strong color to no color) at least the full width of the brush and fade away into the base color. If the color is placed in too tightly, there won't be room to stack other value on top. If a hard line develops, soften it with a clean, damp brush. Side load a ¼-inch (6mm) or ⅜-inch (10mm) angle brush with Mix 6 and side-load float the light value on all of the warm leaves. When the leaves are dry, lighten Mix 6 with more Buttermilk and apply this color on top of the first light value. Apply Mix 10 to all of the cool leaves.

Hint

When applying light values, it's best to use a slightly dryer brush with more paint than when side-load floating in dark values. This will insure better coverage. If the color appears spotty or blotchy, apply another coat of the same color.

4 Apply Light Values to the Flower Petals and Shade Values to the Leaves

Side load a ⅜-inch (10mm) or ⅛-inch (3mm) angle brush with a small amount of Mix 7 and side-load float a shade on the leaves. Repeat with Light Avocado if the shade is too light. When repeating color applications, the second coat should not extend out as far as the first. Allow the color to softly value over the light value. Using an angle brush that fits the areas— a ½-inch (12mm) or ⅜-inch (10mm) on the larger petals and a ¼-inch (6mm) on the smaller petals—lighten rose A by side-load floating Buttermilk on each petal. After the first coat is dry, apply another side-load float of Buttermilk. Side-load float roses B, C, D and E with Mix 4. When dry, repeat. Shade the cool leaves with a side-load float of Mix 8.

back-to-back floats

5 Reinforcing the Shade and Light Values

In this step, continue to side-load float the colors listed below on all the warm leaves and rose petals, using a brush that fits each area. Apply all additional shading and light values within the last application of color; the shade and light value areas should get smaller with each application.

- *Use Mix 5 on the warm leaves. Repeat if needed.*
- *Place a very thin side-load float of Midnite Green at the base of the cool leaves and calyx.*
- *Side-load float Buttermilk on rose A, then lighten Buttermilk with Light Buttermilk. Repeat these applications for better coverage.*
- *Use Mix 4 on roses B, C, D and E, then lighten with Buttermilk and apply again. Repeat using straight Buttermilk.*
- *Side-load float or drybrush Buttermilk in the light areas of the warm leaves to reinforce the light values.*
- *Add a dark value to all of the roses with Mix 1. Make the dark values on the flower petals tighter than on the leaves. When painting soft flowers like these roses, the shadows are smaller and the light values increase.*

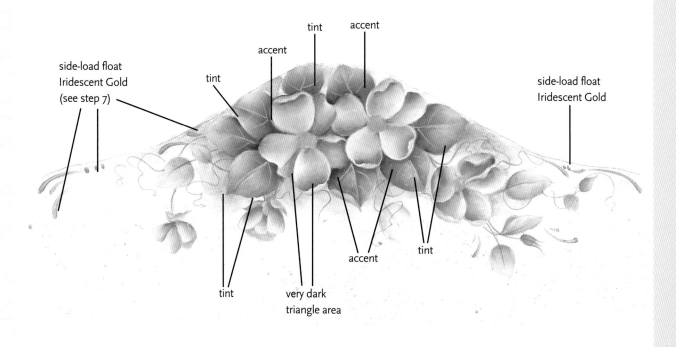

side-load float
Iridescent Gold
(see step 7)

tint

accent

tint

accent

side-load float
Iridescent Gold

tint

very dark
triangle area

accent

tint

6 Adding Details, Accents, Tints, Highlights and Very Dark Values

Float Midnite Green in the triangle areas of the warm leaves. Pick this color up sparingly and use enough water to keep it thin. Side-load float a tint of Mix 1 on both the warm and cool leaves using a ⅜-inch (10mm) angle. Brush mix Antique Rose with a touch of Midnite Green. Add this accent color to the dark value areas of some of the warm leaves. Lighten Taffy Cream with a little Light Buttermilk. Thin this mixture to an ink-like consistency and load on a 10/0 liner. Stay up on the liner brush as you pull the vein lines. When dry, add a highlight of Light Buttermilk + Taffy Cream on all leaves, then drybrush in the center of each light area with Light Buttermilk. Side-load float or drybrush roses A, B and C with a highlight of Light Buttermilk; on roses B and C, the Light Buttermilk may be too warm. Cool the Light Buttermilk by adding a touch of Taffy Cream to it. Add tints to some of the petals with Blue Mist.

Add a touch more dark in the triangle areas or under the flips with Antique Rose. Pull the vines and stems with a liner brush and Mix 5 thinned with water. If more darks are needed close to the objects, deepen the dark areas in the background with very thin Midnite Green.

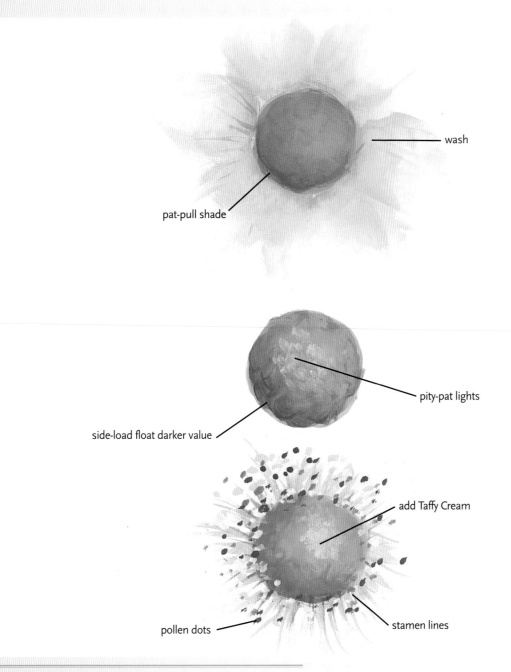

wash

pat-pull shade

pity-pat lights

side-load float darker value

add Taffy Cream

pollen dots

stamen lines

7 Finishing the Project

Wash over the petals behind the centers of the roses with very thin Cadmium Yellow. Shade the lower left side of the rose centers with a pat-pull side-load float (lay the brush down and set the color in, then lift and pat in again) of Light Avocado + a touch of Cadmium Yellow. Repeat. When dry, apply the light value to the right side of the rose centers with Cadmium Yellow + a touch of Taffy Cream and pity-pat the color out toward the shade. When dry, lighten the Cadmium Yellow with more Taffy Cream and pat on top of the last light value. Side-load float a mixture of half Light Avocado + half Midnite Green over the shade area to deepen the lower left side. Using a liner and a thinned mixture of Cadmium Yellow + a touch of Light

Avocado, pull stamen lines out from the center; keep some very short and make some longer. When dry, add pollen dots in and around the center using Antique Rose, Cadmium Yellow and Taffy Cream. To finish the design, add Iridescent Gold strokework with a liner brush. You may need to thin this paint with water to get the proper consistency for strokework. Spatter the lower portion of the towel holder, the edges, brackets and pole with Iridescent Gold. Side-load float a wash of Iridescent Gold over the edges. When dry, use a 1-inch (25mm) wash brush to apply several coats of J.W. etc. Right-Step Matte Varnish over the entire piece. Reassemble and enjoy!

Spring *Pansies*
on a Potpourri Bowl

In Victorian times, pansies represented friendship. They have always been one of my favorite flowers to paint. The range of colors, from rich purples to soft pastels, adds variety to any design. This bowl provides a functional as well as decorative piece. If you'd prefer a different surface, the ring of pansies can be separated and painted on a box top, hand mirror—the choices are endless. In this lesson you will learn to **create petals that are triangular in shape.**

Color Mixes

Mix 1
1 part Hauser Light Green + 1 part Soft Grey

Mix 2
1 part Pink Chiffon + 1 part Orchid

Mix 3
1 part Violet Ice + 1 part Country Blue

Mix 4
1 part Violet Haze + 1 part Wisteria

Mix 5
2 parts Midnite Green + 1 part Silver Sage Green

Mix 6
1 part Mix 1 + 1 part Titanium White

Mix 7
1 part Mix 6 + 1 part Titanium White

Mix 8
1 part Orchid + 1 part Plum

Mix 9
1 part Deep Periwinkle + 1 part Country Blue

Mix 10
1 part Wisteria + 1 part Titanium White

Mix 11
2 parts Plum + 1 part Orchid

Mix 12
1 part Deep Periwinkle + 1 part Payne's Grey

Mix 13
1 part Pansy Lavender + 2 parts Vintage Wine

Mix 14
1 part Yellow Light + 1 part Pineapple + a dot of Vintage Wine

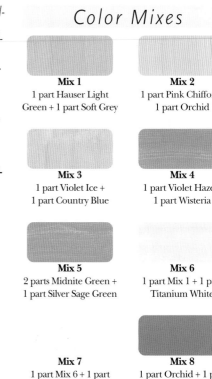

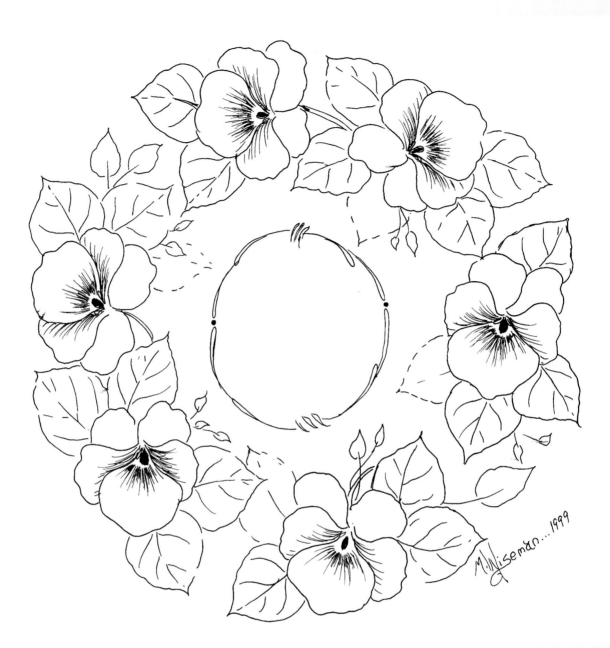

M.Wiseman...1999

This pattern may be hand-traced or photocopied for personal use only. Enlarge at 154% on a photocopier to return to full size.

Materials

Surface

- This 9¼" (23.5cm) diameter metal bowl is available from Barb Watson Brushworks, P.O. Box 1467, Moreno Valley, CA 92556. Phone: (909) 653-3780. Web site: www.barbwatson.com.

DecoArt Americana Acrylic Paints

- Alizarin Crimson DA179
- Black Plum DA172
- Country Blue DA41
- Deep Periwinkle DA212
- Hauser Light Green DA131
- Hauser Medium Green DA132
- Midnite Green DA84
- Orchid DA33
- Pansy Lavender DA154
- Payne's Grey DA167
- Pineapple DA6
- Pink Chiffon DA192
- Plum DA175
- Silver Sage Green DA149
- Soft Black DA155
- Taupe DA109
- Titanium White DA1
- Violet Haze DA197
- Wisteria DA211
- Yellow Light DA144

Delta Ceramcoat Acrylic Paints

- Soft Grey 02515
- Vintage Wine 02434
- Violet Ice 02557

Brushes

- ⅜-inch (10mm), ½-inch (12mm) and ⅝-inch (15mm) angle brushes
- 10/0 script liner
- 1-inch (25mm) polyfoam brush
- no. 2 round

Additional Supplies

- tracing paper
- gray transfer paper
- 320-grit wet/dry sandpaper
- tack rag
- wet palette or paint pots
- Americana Acrylic Sealer/Finisher DAS13, matte

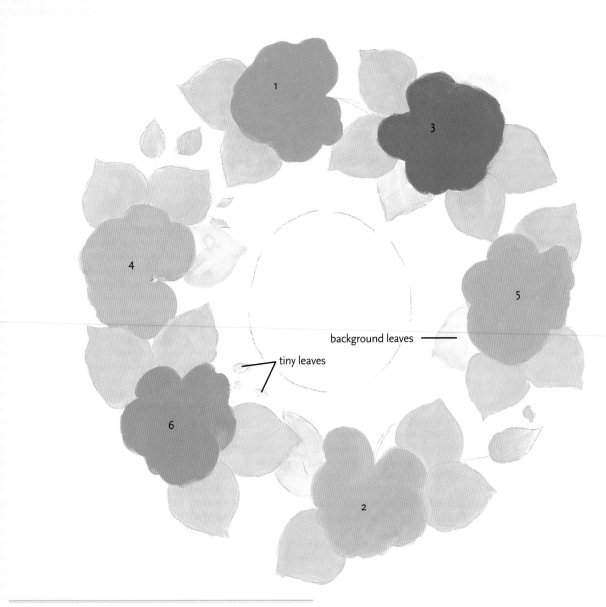

background leaves

tiny leaves

1 Preparing the Surface and Basecoating the Pansies and Leaves

This metal bowl comes pre-primed with a metal primer. Wipe the entire bowl with a tack rag to remove any dust or oily fingerprints. Basecoat across the bowl with a 1-inch (25mm) polyfoam brush loaded with Soft Grey. When dry, apply a second coat, stroking in the same direction. Sand lightly and wipe with a tack rag. Apply a third coat to achieve opaque coverage. Transfer only the main pattern outline with gray transfer paper; the details are easier to paint freehand using the pattern as a guide. Using a fully loaded ⅝-inch (15mm) angle brush, block in the flowers and leaves using the colors listed below and at right. Each object may require more than one coat to achieve opaque coverage; dry between coats. Base the pansies in as a whole, not as individual petals.

- *Block in the yellow-green leaves with Mix 1.*
- *Base pansy 1 with Orchid.*
- *Base pansy 2 with Mix 2.*
- *Base pansy 3 with Mix 4.*
- *Base pansy 4 with Wisteria.*
- *Base pansy 5 with Deep Periwinkle.*
- *Base pansy 6 with Mix 3.*
- *Using a no. 2 round loaded with Silver Sage Green, block in all of the tiny leaves.*
- *Load a ½-inch (12mm) angle brush with a wash of Silver Sage Green and apply to the background leaves indicated with broken lines on the pattern.*

2 Creating the Background Shadow Foliage

Side load a ⅝-inch (15mm) angle brush with a wash of Silver Sage Green. Place the long edge of the brush next to the design and pat-pull the color away from the design. The color should fade away toward the top of the bowl on one side of the design and toward the bottom of the bowl on the other side of the design. When dry, repeat the wash of Silver Sage Green on top of the first layer, keeping it closer to the elements in the design. Deepen the triangle areas with a wash of Mix 5. Place accents of Plum, Vintage Wine, Midnite Green, Deep Periwinkle and Payne's Grey into areas of the background

where the flowers or leaves are touching. Add soft tints of Pineapple, Pink Chiffon and Violet Ice to the areas where the Silver Sage Green touches the background. Apply these tints and accents with thin color side loaded on a ½-inch (12mm) angle brush, patting into the area where the color is desired. The colors I've listed are suggestions; not all of the colors need to be used. You can add the tints as you're painting the design or after the flowers and leaves are complete.

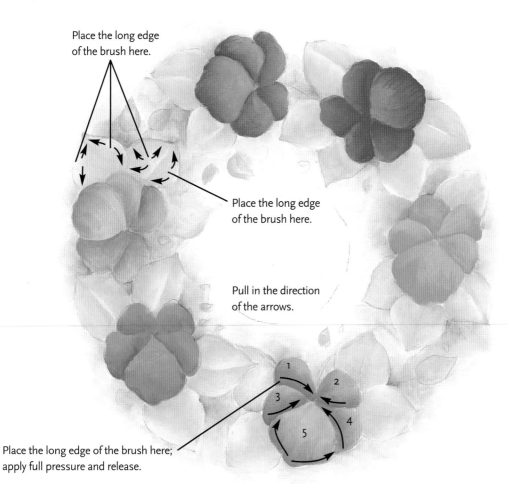

Place the long edge of the brush here.

Place the long edge of the brush here.

Pull in the direction of the arrows.

Place the long edge of the brush here; apply full pressure and release.

3 Applying Shade Values to the Flowers and Light Values to the Leaves

Use gray transfer paper to apply the pattern detail lines, if needed. Using a ½-inch (12mm) angle brush, side-load float Mix 6 in the light areas of all yellow-green leaves. Reload the brush after each application. Place the light values on both outside edges of each leaf, or on one side of the vein line and along the leaf edge on the other side. Lay the brush down in the center of the largest area, pull the color toward the base of the leaf and release the pressure on the brush as you pull. The color should fade off as the area gets smaller. Flip the brush over, lay it on the edge of the first placement and pull the brush toward the tip of the leaf. Again, release the pressure on the brush as you pull, making the color fade as the area gets smaller. When the first light application is dry, use a smaller brush to apply a second light value with Mix 7. Apply this color on top of the previous side-load float, keeping it within the previous color. Apply the shade values to the pansy petals with a side-load float of the colors listed at right. Use an angle brush, reloading after each application. Start with petal 1 and work around to petal 5. The shade color should blend and fade into the base color and should cover about three-quarters of the

petal area. Apply full pressure in the largest area of the petal and release the pressure as the petal gets tighter. On petals 1 through 4, lay the long edge of the brush along the edge of the petal nearest to the petal on top of it. On the fifth petal, place the long edge of the brush in the middle of the top edge and pull toward the side. Replace the brush in the middle of the top edge, slightly overlapping the previous stroke, and again pull toward the side of the petal. Release the pressure as you pull the brush across the petal, allowing the color to cover a smaller area. Apply a second coat of this color when the first is dry.

- Shade pansy 1 with Orchid.
- Shade pansy 2 with Mix 8.
- Shade pansy 3 with Pansy Lavender.
- Shade pansy 4 with Violet Haze.
- Shade pansy 5 with Country Blue.
- Shade pansy 6 with Mix 9.

4 Applying Shade Values to the Leaves and Light Values to the Pansies

Using a ½-inch (12mm) angle brush, shade all of the yellow-green leaves with a side-load float of Hauser Light Green. Lay the brush at the base of the leaf and pull toward the tip. Place the shade in with a back-to-back float on the leaves that have light on both outside edges. To do this, place the long edge of the brush in the center next to the vein. Pull one side, then flip the brush over and pull in the shade on the other side. On the leaves with light on one side of the vein, side-load float the shade color on the other side of the vein, allowing it to fade over to the light edge. Then side-load float the color along the outer leaf edge, fading toward the light vein area and over the light areas slightly. Side-load float the light values on the pansies with a ½-inch (12mm) angle loaded with the colors listed at right. Place the long edge of the brush on the outside edge of the petal. Start in the largest area and pull toward the tight

area, releasing the brush as you pull. On the fifth petal, pull the light value across the petal, keeping the long edge of the brush toward the back petals. Stop in the center, flip the brush over and pull again to the center; release as this stroke overlaps the last. Allow the application of color to dry and apply the same color again, keeping the color within the previous application.

- *Apply the light value to pansy 1 with Pink Chiffon.*
- *Apply the light value to pansy 2 with Mix 10.*
- *Apply the light value to pansy 3 with Wisteria.*
- *Apply the light value to pansy 4 with Mix 11.*
- *Apply the light value to pansy 5 with Violet Ice.*
- *Apply the light value to pansy 6 with Mix 12.*

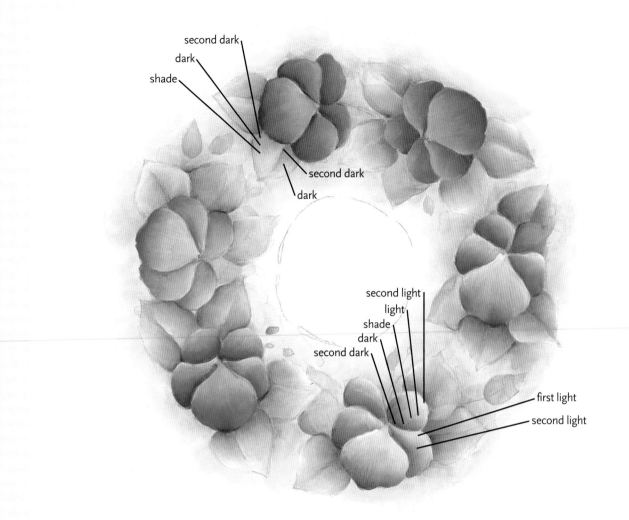

second dark
dark
shade
second dark
dark

second light
light
shade
dark
second dark
first light
second light

5 Building the Light and Dark Values on the Pansies and Leaves

In this step, continue to side-load float the colors listed below and at right on all of the leaves and flowers. Choose a brush that fits each area. When applying the colors, stay within the last application of color each time a new color is applied. It's helpful to use a smaller brush or load less color across the brush as the areas of application get smaller. Side-load float the leaves with Hauser Medium Green. When dry, side-load float in the darkest areas with Midnite Green. When the dark areas are complete, side-load float a highlight in the light area with Titanium White. Also side-load float the background leaves with a wash of Midnite Green. Wash over these leaves with thinned Soft Grey if they appear too harsh. Deepen the shade areas on the pansies with the first color listed below and at right. When that color is dry, apply the next dark value listed. Each shade value can be applied more than once to increase the depth of color.

- Deepen the shade on pansy 1 with Mix 11, then Plum.
- Deepen the shade on pansy 2 with Plum, then Black Plum.

- Deepen the shade on pansy 3 with Vintage Wine; redeepen with more Vintage Wine.
- Deepen the shade on pansy 4 with Mix 13, then Vintage Wine.
- Deepen the shade on pansy 5 with Mix 12, then Payne's Grey.
- Deepen the shade on pansy 6 with Deep Periwinkle, then Mix 12.

Side-load float the lightest value on each of the petals using the colors listed below. The same color may be repeated or can be lightened with Titanium White if a stronger light is desired.

- The lightest value for pansy 1 is Pink Chiffon + Titanium White.
- The lightest value for pansy 2 is Pink Chiffon.
- The lightest value for pansy 3 is Wisteria.
- The lightest value for pansy 4 is Wisteria + Titanium White.
- The lightest value for pansy 5 is Violet Ice.
- The lightest value for pansy 6 is Violet Ice + Titanium White.

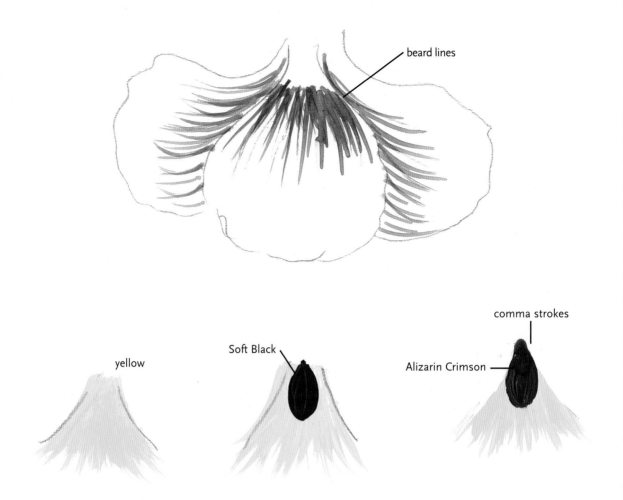

beard lines

yellow

Soft Black

comma strokes

Alizarin Crimson

6 *The Pansy Centers and Beards*

Using a small round or liner, pull in the center area with Mix 14. When dry, place in a press dot of Soft Black. When this is dry, add a dot on top with Alizarin Crimson. Place comma strokes on both sides of the black press dot with Titanium White + a touch of Pineapple, allowing the strokes to fade into the outside edge of the fifth petal. Add the beards to the pansies using a liner brush loaded with the appropriate color listed below, thinned with water to an ink-like consistency. Pull the color down into the center of the petal and away from the large petals on the side.

- *Use Soft Black + Black Plum on pansies 1 and 2.*
- *Use Soft Black + Vintage Wine on pansies 3 and 4.*
- *Use Soft Black + Payne's Grey on pansies 5 and 6.*

7 *Adding Details, Accents and Tints*

Load a 10/0 liner brush with thinned Titanium White mixed with a touch of Hauser Light Green and place in all of the vein lines on the yellow-green leaves. Side-load float Orchid in the light areas of some leaves as a tint. Side-load float Plum, Vintage Wine or Payne's Grey in the middle or dark value areas of some of the leaves as an accent color. Side-load float a wash of Plum or Black Plum in the darkest areas of the purple pansies as an accent color. Side-load float a wash of Vintage Wine in the darkest areas of the pink and blue pansies. These accent colors will tie the design together. Outline the leaves in the background using a liner brush loaded with

Mix 5 thinned with water. Add a touch of Hauser Medium Green to Mix 5 to warm it up and pull in the vines, tendrils and pansy stems. Lighten the centers of the pansy stems with Silver Sage Green. Side-load float Midnite Green at the ends for a shade. Stroke in the commas on the bottom of the bowl using Silver Sage Green. Place the dots in with Taupe. Finish the bowl with Americana Acrylic Sealer/Finisher. Two or three light coats are sufficient to give a protective finish to the surface. Fill the bottom of the bowl with your favorite potpourri and enjoy your artwork and the pleasant aroma.

Pink *Geraniums*
on a Pie Carrier Basket

Geraniums are a popular summer plant all over the country. The flowers—which range in color from scarlet red to white— are interesting to paint with their round leaves and groups of five-petaled florets. In this lesson you will learn to **use values to define a group of petals, as well as individual flowers.**

You will be painting with a complementary color scheme of red and green. You will learn how to use a color's complement to cool its intensity.

The sphere-shaped leaves, with the addition of accents, provide a challenge in creating form and add interest to the design.

Color Mixes

Mix 1
3 parts Olive Green +
1 part Light Avocado

Mix 2
1 part Jade Green +
1 part Eggshell

Mix 3
5 parts Deep Burgundy +
1 part Eggshell

Mix 4
3 parts Mix 3 +
1 part Eggshell

Mix 5
2 parts Mix 4 +
1 part Eggshell

Mix 6
1 part Mix 5 +
1 part Eggshell

Mix 7
1 part Mix 6 + 1 part
Titanium White

Mix 8
8 parts Deep Burgundy +
1 part Black Green

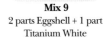

Mix 9
2 parts Eggshell + 1 part
Titanium White

Mix 10
2 parts Light Avocado +
1 part Jade Green

Mix 11
2 parts Avocado + 1 part
Black Green

This pattern may be hand-traced or photocopied for personal use only. Enlarge at 222% on a photocopier to return to full size.

Materials

Surface

- This 13½" × 11½" × 5¾" (34.3cm × 29.2cm × 14.6cm) single pie carrier basket (item no. WD7515) is available from Hofcraft, P.O. Box 72-W, Grand Haven, MI 49417. Phone: (616) 847-8822. Web site: www.hofcraft.com. E-mail: hofcraft@hofcraft.com.

DecoArt Americana Acrylic Paints

- Avocado DA52
- Black Green DA157
- Deep Burgundy DA128
- Eggshell DA153
- Ice Blue DA135
- Jade Green DA57
- Light Avocado DA106
- Olive Green DA56
- Shale Green DA152
- Taffy Cream DA5
- Titanium White DA1
- Yellow Light DA144

Brushes

- no. 1 round
- no. 6 fabric round
- 1-inch (25mm) wash brush
- mop brush
- ¼-inch (6mm), ⅜-inch (10mm), ½-inch (12mm), ⅝-inch (15mm), ¾-inch (19mm) and 1-inch (25mm) angle brushes
- no. 10/0 liner
- polyfoam brush

Additional Supplies

- tracing paper
- black or gray transfer paper
- 320-grit wet/dry sandpaper
- tack rag
- wet palette or paint pots
- Designs From the Heart Wood Sealer
- J.W. etc. Right-Step Matte Varnish

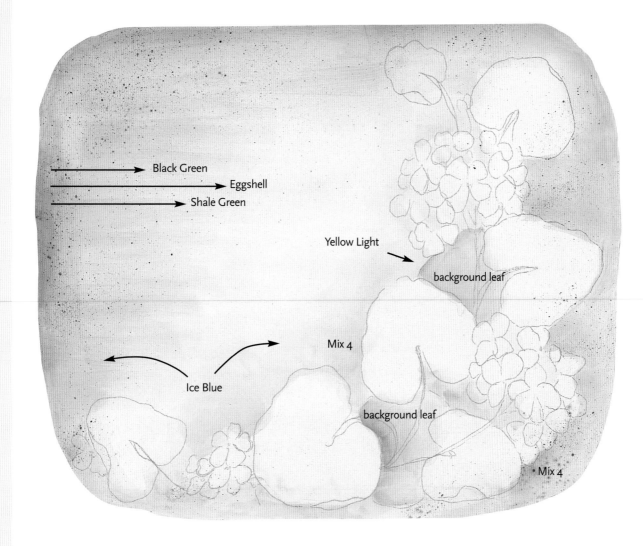

Black Green

Eggshell

Shale Green

Yellow Light

background leaf

Mix 4

Ice Blue

background leaf

Mix 4

1 *Preparing the Surface and Creating the Background*

Seal both sides of the basket lid with one coat of Designs From the Heart Wood Sealer. When dry, sand with 320-grit sandpaper and wipe off the dust with a tack rag. Mix 2 parts Titanium White + 1 part Eggshell and apply two coats to the top of the lid, allowing the first coat to dry before applying the next. Sand lightly between coats, if needed. Thin the above mix with water to a medium wash. Dampen the woven part of the basket with clean water and apply the thinned mix over the woven areas. When dry, the woven areas can be stained again if a whiter stain is desired. Paint the handles, basket rim and the inside of the lid Black Green; three or more coats will be needed for opaque coverage. Sand lightly between coats to keep the paint smooth. Next, thin Black Green with water and load on a no. 6 fabric round. Spatter the lid and basket. When dry, spatter again with thinned Mix 8. Transfer the main design

lines; the details can be added later or freehanded. Apply side-load washes of Eggshell, Shale Green and Black Green to the background, using a large angle brush that fits the area to which you're applying the color. Apply the Eggshell first, fading it out the furthest from the design. Next apply Shale Green within the Eggshell application. Apply the Black Green over the Shale Green, keeping it very thin and applying it several times to keep the background soft. Add tints to some of the background areas as shown using side-load washes of Yellow Light, Ice Blue and Mix 4. Wash over the background leaves with Shale Green and side-load float with a wash of Black Green + Jade Green.

---

2 *Basecoating the Flowers, Leaves and Stems*

Using a fully loaded ⅝-inch (15mm) angle brush, block in the leaves, using the colors listed below. Use a ⅜-inch (10mm) angle for the flower petals. Each object may require more than one coat to achieve opaque coverage.

- *Block in leaves A, B, C and D with Mix 1.*
- *Block in leaves E, F and G with Mix 2.*
- *Block in the top flower's center petals with Mix 7 and the right and left petals with Mix 6.*
- *Block in the center petals on the lower right flower with Mix 6 and the outside petals with Mix 5.*
- *Block in the petals on the lower left with Mix 7.*
- *Using a liner brush or a no. 1 round loaded with Mix 1, pull in the leaf and flower stems.*

3 Applying Shade Values to the Flowers and Light Values to the Leaves

Using a ⅝-inch (15mm) angle brush, side-load float Olive Green in the center of leaves A, B, C and D. Apply leaves E, F and G using Eggshell side loaded on a ½-inch (12mm) angle brush. Lay the long edge of the brush down in the middle of the leaf and pat-pull the color toward the outside edge, going around the leaf. Flip the brush over and lay it on the edge of the first placement. Pat-pull, allowing the color to fade into the inside of the leaf, again going all the way around the leaf. Where the area of application is smaller, place less pressure on the brush. Where the area is larger, use full pressure. When dry, apply another light value to leaves A, B, C and D with Mix 9. Repeat the Eggshell on leaves E, F and G, placing the color on top of and staying within the first application. Each color can be repeated for better coverage. Apply the shade to each petal with a ⅜-inch (10mm) angle brush and a side-load float of the appropriate color listed at right. Apply the color to

the petals in the back first, then to the petals that are on top. Only a few florets in each group have full five-petal blossoms; the rest should have only two or three petals showing, or only a portion of some petals visible. On all the foreground and midground petals, apply the shade near the center and to separate the petals. Cover about half of the petal with shade color, then fade it into the base color. On petals far in the background, cover the entire petal so it will recede. The same color may be applied twice.

- Use Mix 5 to shade petals basecoated with Mix 7.
- Use Mix 4 to shade petals basecoated with Mix 6.
- Use Mix 3 to shade petals basecoated with Mix 5.

4 Applying Shade Values to Leaves and Light Values to the Blossoms

Apply shade values on leaves A, B, C and D with a side-load float of Light Avocado, loaded on a ⅝-inch (15mm) or ¾-inch (19mm) angle brush. Use Mix 10 to shade leaves E, F and G. Apply the color all the way around the leaf edge and fade it in toward the light area. Flip the brush over and side-load float all the way around the stem area, allowing the color to fade slightly toward the light area on both sides. This color may be side-load floated twice for better coverage. Side-load float the light values on the petals with one value lighter than the base color, as listed at right, using a brush that fits the area. Allow the color to fade toward the shade area, but not into it. Some of the petals way in the back will not receive a light value. When dry, apply the light values again for better coverage. If needed, the colors can be lightened by adding Titanium White or using a lighter mix.

- *Brush mix a small amount of Titanium White into Mix 7 to lighten petals basecoated with Mix 7.*
- *Use Mix 7 to lighten petals basecoated with Mix 6.*
- *Use Mix 6 to lighten petals basecoated with Mix 5.*

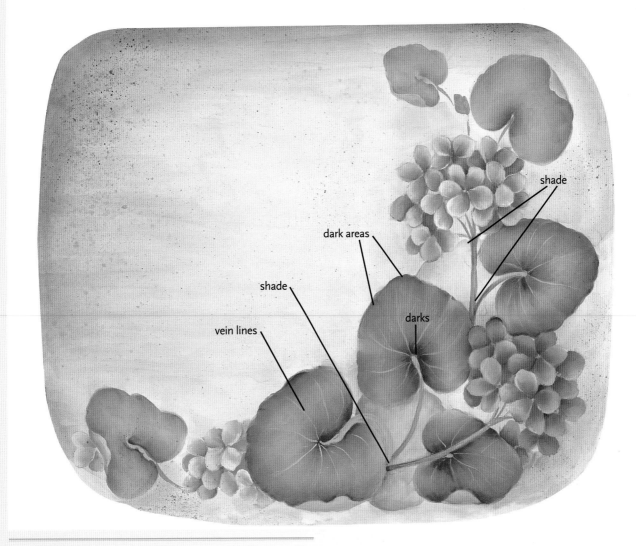

shade

dark areas

shade

darks

vein lines

5 Building Light and Dark Values on the Geraniums and Leaves

In this step, continue to side-load float the appropriate colors on all of the leaves and geranium petals using a brush that fits each area. When applying the colors, stay within the last application of color each time another color is applied. It's helpful to use a smaller brush or load less color across the brush as the areas of application get smaller. Add lighter values to leaves A, B, C and D with Eggshell. Add a second light with Eggshell + a touch of Titanium White. On leaves marked E, F and G, side-load float a light value with Mix 9 + Titanium White. On leaves marked A, B, C and D, side-load float an Avocado dark value on all the areas where the shade was applied. When dry, deepen the areas where the leaf protrudes, in the stem area and under any flips with Mix 11. Repeat Mix 11 in the tight areas for a deeper shadow. Deepen the shadow areas on leaves E, F and G with Light Avocado + a touch of Black Green. Repeat this color in any of the darkest areas. Using a liner and Eggshell + a touch of Olive Green thinned with water, add vein lines to leaves A, B, C and D. Deepen the flower petals with the first color listed below; when that color is dry, apply the next color.

- *Use Mix 5 to deepen the petals basecoated with Mix 7. Deepen further with Mix 4.*
- *Use Mix 4 to deepen the petals basecoated with Mix 6. Deepen further with Mix 3.*
- *Use Mix 3 to deepen the petals basecoated with Mix 5. Deepen further with Mix 3 + Mix 8.*

Lighten the light value on the flower petals using a lighter value or by adding Titanium White to lighten. Give the petals in the center of the group another value that is lighter than the last one used. Shade the stems at the base and sides with a side-load float of Light Avocado. Using a liner brush loaded with Taffy Cream, drag through the center of the stems to create a light value.

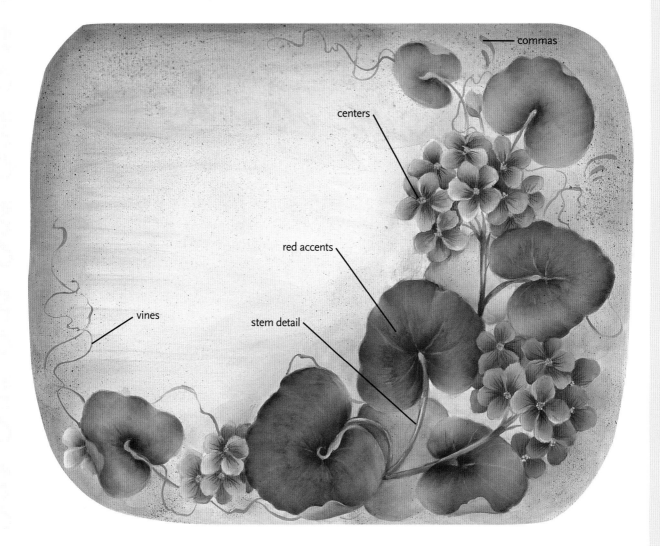

commas

centers

red accents

vines

stem detail

6 Adding Details, Accents and Tints

If the leaves need more highlights, float Taffy Cream in the lightest area and deepen the area between the vein lines with Mix 11 + Black Green. Using Mix 8 side loaded on a ½-inch (12mm) angle brush, skizzle a back-to-back float in the red lines on the leaves. Place this over the light area of leaves A, B and D and in the stem area of the other leaves. Mop lightly to soften or blend out if needed. Wash tints of Mix 3 on the two background leaves. Add Mix 8 to Avocado and shade the stems again. Pull all vines with a mix of Jade Green + Light Avocado and a liner brush. Using a liner brush loaded with Taffy Cream, drag across the vines here and there to create light areas. Pull the comma strokes in with a liner brush loaded with Jade Green. Add stamen lines to the petals near the center using a 10/0 liner brush. Use thinned Mix 8 on the darker petals and Deep Burgundy on the light flower petals.

Pull the lines from the center out, creating about five lines on each of the petals that have centers. Place the flower centers in with a large dot of Mix 1. Add smaller dots with the tip of the liner brush and Olive Green + Eggshell.

7 Completing the Pie Carrier

Using a 1-inch (25mm) wash brush, apply several coats of
J.W. etc. Right-Step Matte Varnish to the lid. You don't need to
varnish the woven areas of the basket. Add a fabric liner if desired. At your next summer party, this pie carrier will receive as
many compliments as the dish you carry in it. Enjoy!

Victorian *Roses* on a Stationery Box

Roses are the favorite flower of the decorative artist, maybe in part because they present a challenge to paint. In this lesson you will learn, step by step, the strokes that **build a beautiful stroke rose.** All stroke roses are completed following the method shown on pages 60-62. Only the color will change.

We will also create filler flowers to add to our composition, stressing stroke and color harmony.

Color Mixes

Mix 1
10 parts White + 1 part Taffy Cream

Mix 2
1 part Royal Purple + 1 part Black Plum

Mix 3
1 part Mauve + 1 part French Mauve

Mix 4
2 parts Light Avocado + 1 part Black Green

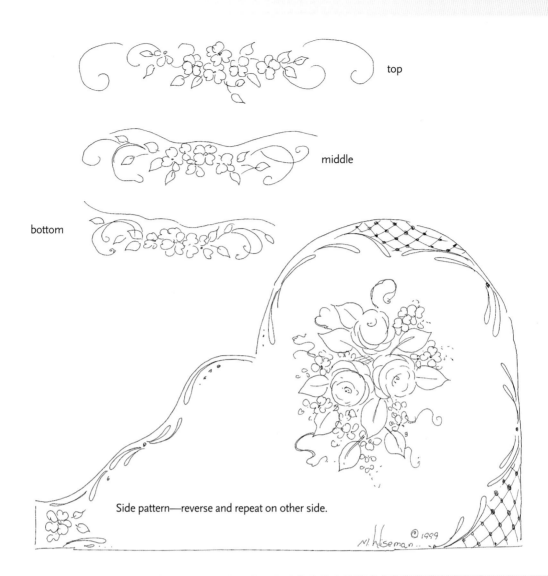

top

middle

bottom

Side pattern—reverse and repeat on other side.

© 1999
M. Wiseman

This pattern may be hand-traced or photocopied for personal use only. Enlarge at 200% on a photocopier to return to full size.

Materials

Surface
- This 11" × 12" × 7¼" (27.9cm × 30.5cm × 18.4cm) stationery box is available from The Cutting Edge, 343 Twin Pines Dr., Glendale, OR 97442. Phone: (909) 464-0440.

DecoArt Americana Acrylic Paints
- Antique Mauve DA162
- Black Green DA157
- Black Plum DA172
- Cranberry Wine DA112
- Eggshell DA153
- French Mauve DA186
- Jade Green DA57
- Light Avocado DA106
- Mauve DA26
- Reindeer Moss Green DA187
- Royal Purple DA150
- Shale Green DA152
- Taffy Cream DA5
- Titanium White DA1
- True Ochre DA143

Golden Acrylics
- Iridescent Gold Deep

Brushes
- ⅛-inch (3mm), ¼-inch (6mm), ⅜-inch (10mm), ½-inch (12mm), ¾-inch (19mm) and 1-inch (25mm) angle brushes
- no. 10/0 liner
- no. 2 and no. 6 filberts
- 1-inch (25mm) polyfoam brush
- 1-inch (25mm) wash brush

Additional Supplies
- tracing paper
- black or gray transfer paper
- 320-grit wet/dry sandpaper
- tack rag
- wet palette or paint pots
- sea sponge
- J.W. etc. White Lightning
- J.W. etc. Right-Step Matte Varnish

lid pattern

top

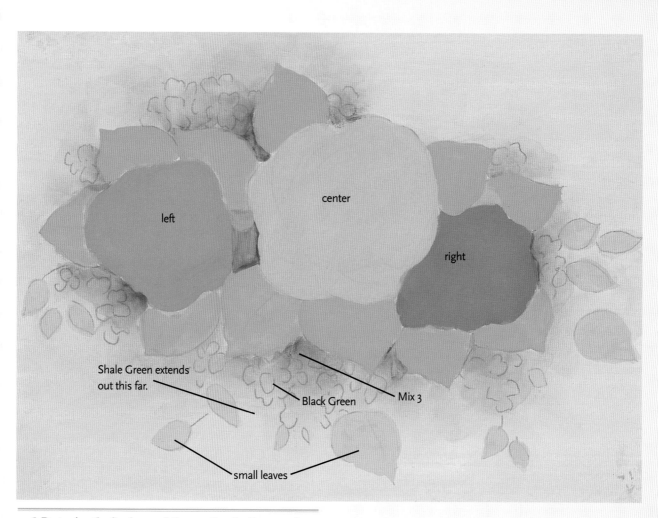

left

center

right

Shale Green extends
out this far.

Black Green

Mix 3

small leaves

1 Preparing the Surface and Basecoating the Roses on the Lid

Using a polyfoam brush, apply one coat of White Lightning to the entire piece. When dry, sand with 320-grit sandpaper and wipe the dust off with a tack rag. Next, apply two coats of Eggshell to the entire piece, allowing the first coat to dry and sanding lightly before applying another coat. Thin Titanium White with water and apply a very thin wash over all the Eggshell areas. Transfer the design to the surface using black or gray transfer paper. Wet a small sea sponge with clean water and dip it into Iridescent Gold Deep. Press the sponge several times onto the palette to work the color into the sponge. With a brush loaded with clean water, wet the background of the front, back and sides of the box. Press the sponge onto the wet areas. Rinse and reload the sponge when necessary. Sponge gold in the corners of the lid, fading in toward the design. Side-load float the edges of the lid and sides with Iridescent Gold Deep on a 1-inch (25mm) angle brush. Allow the color to fade toward the design. Dampen the background with water and side load a ¾-inch (19mm) angle brush with Shale Green. Side-load float this color around the design, allowing it to fade out beyond the design elements. Apply a second shade on top of the Shale Green with a side-load wash of Black Green. When dry, add a side-load wash of Royal Purple on top of the Black Green areas. Using an angle brush that fits the area, block in the following items using the colors listed. Apply two coats for opaque coverage, drying between applications.

- *Block in the center rose with French Mauve.*
- *Block in the right rose with Mauve.*
- *Block in the left rose with Mix 3.*
- *Block in the large leaves with Jade Green.*
- *Block in the small leaves with Reindeer Moss Green.*

2 Basecoating the Roses and Leaves on the Sides of the Box

Using a ⅜-inch (10mm) angle fully loaded with Mauve, block in the small roses on the sides of the box. When dry, apply a second coat. Using a no. 6 filbert loaded with Reindeer Moss Green, base in all the leaves around the roses. With Reindeer Moss Green and a no. 2 filbert, place in the leaves on the three border designs on the front sections.

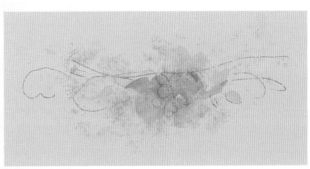

border designs on front sections

3 *Applying the Shade Values to the Leaves and Roses*

Side load a ½-inch (12mm) angle brush with thinned Jade Green and side-load float into the Light Avocado shade areas on all of the large leaves. Shade the small leaves with a thin side-load float of Light Avocado. When dry, apply a second side load float of Light Avocado to deepen the shade areas of the leaves. Shade the roses with a side-load float of the colors listed at right, applying the color to the base of the "ball" of the rose, to the inside center and under each of the outside petals to separate them. Repeat when dry.

- *Shade the center rose with Mauve.*
- *Shade the right rose with Antique Mauve + a touch of Cranberry Wine.*
- *Shade the left rose with Antique Mauve.*

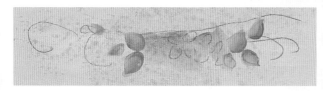

4 *Apply Shade Values to the Leaves and Roses on the Sides*

Using a ⅜-inch (10mm) angle brush, shade the roses with a side-load float of Antique Mauve. Side load a ⅜-inch (10mm) angle brush and side-load float thinned Light Avocado to the base of the leaves and down the vein areas.

5 Apply Light Values to the Leaves and Roses on the Top of the Box

Side-load float Jade Green in all the light areas, allowing the color to fade into the edges of the shade areas. Floating Jade Green will soften any shadows that may have faded out too far and give the leaf a soft, blended appearance. When dry, side-load float Reindeer Moss Green in the light areas of the large leaves. Float the small leaves at the tips with a brush mix of Reindeer Moss Green + Titanium White. Using a liner and thinned Reindeer Moss Green + a touch of Titanium White, line in the vein lines. Place the rose petals in as shown on pages 60-62 using a lighter value of color. Dress the brush in the appropriate base color and side load the lighter value of color. Starting at the back of the rose, pull in the strokes to create petals. Continue with the same color and strokes for the petals in the front of the rose, then finally the outer petals.

Dress and load the brush before each stroke.

- *Use Mix 1 for the petals on the center rose.*
- *Use Mix 3 for the petals on the right rose.*
- *Use French Mauve for the petals on the left rose.*

6 Dress the brush with the base color (French Mauve) and side load into the light mix (Mix 1). Stroke in the back center petal with a C-stroke.

7 Stroke a comma stroke to the right of the back center petal.

8 Stroke another comma to the left of the back center petal.

9 Drop down to begin the second row of inside petals. The fourth stroke straddles the two petals behind it.

10 Place the fifth stroke on the other side of petal 4.

11 Drop down slightly below row 2 and stroke in the sixth petal.

12 Stroke on petal 7.

13 Drop down slightly and stroke in petal 8.

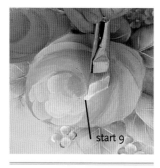   

14 Start the ninth stroke up on the chisel edge in front of the throat of the rose; as you pull the brush, begin to lay it down.

15 The brush hairs are all touching the surface here.

16 Release the ninth stroke up on the chisel edge of the brush.

17 Pull the tenth stroke into the ball on the left side.

18 Complete stroke 10 up on the chisel edge.

19 Stroke petal 11 on the left side.

20 End stroke 12 on the chisel edge under the ball of the rose.

21 Begin stroke 13.

22 End stroke 13 at the ball base and number 12 stroke.

23 Stroke in petal 14 under stroke 12.

24 Stroke petal 15 under stroke 13, ending between stroke 12 and 14.

25 Stroke in 16 under stroke 14 and 15.

26 Begin stroke 17 just below the stroke in front of the bowl. Lay the brush flat in the center. Pull the brush, releasing the hairs off the surface as you pull.

27 End stroke 17 up on the chisel edge.

28 Repeat for stroke 18.

29 Side-load float the shade value and float across the back petals.

30 Side-load float inside the bowl of the rose.

31 Side-load float at the base of the rose. Start in the center and pull off at the edge.

32 Repeat the side-load float on the other side of the bowl.

33 Side-load float a thin shade under each of the lower petals to separate.

34 Using a small angle brush, side load into the highlight mix and lighten the top edge of the light strokes.

35 Add highlights to all the back petals.

36 Chisel in highlight strokes to the front of the bowl.

37 Highlight strokes continued.

38 Continue to highlight the lower petals.

39 Reinforce the darks inside the bowl.

40 Float a shade on the outer edge of the petal.

41 Using a liner brush loaded with True Ochre, scatter dots in the bowl center. Then add dots of Taffy Cream.

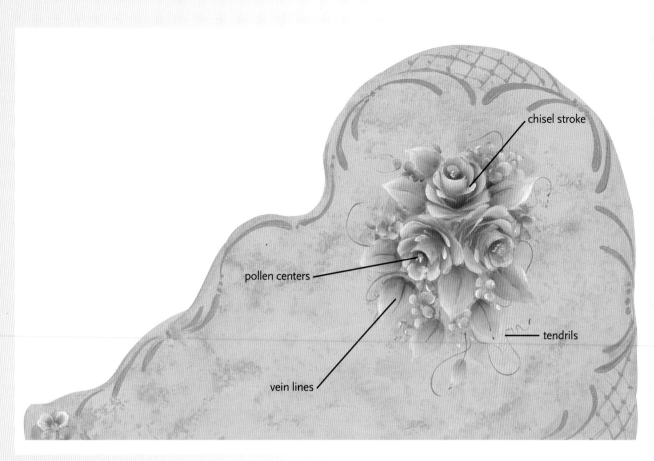

chisel stroke

pollen centers

tendrils

vein lines

Example of three borders on front section.

42 Apply the Light Strokes to the Roses and Light Values to the Leaves

Lighten the leaves with a float of Reindeer Moss Green + Titanium White. Repeat when dry. Deepen the shade areas of the leaves with a thinned side-load float of Mix 2. Line in the vein lines with a brush mix of Light Avocado and Royal Purple loaded on a liner brush. Using the same mix, add tendrils to the outer area of the design. Dress a ¼-inch (6mm) angle brush with French Mauve and touch into Mix 1. Stroke in the back petals first, then the side petals and finally the center petals. Redress and reload the brush after every stroke. Holding the brush perpendicular to the surface, place in the small petals in the center by pulling on the chisel edge of the brush. Apply a dark value to the base of the rose and in the center with a side-load float of thinned Cranberry Wine. Scatter dots of True Ochre on the centers, then add lighter dots of Taffy Cream. Stroke in the linework on the sides with Iridescent Gold Deep thinned slightly with water and loaded on a liner brush.

tendrils

strokes

side-load float
darkest shade

accent color

43 Adding Dark Values and Accent Colors to the Leaves and Creating Filler Flowers

Deepen the shade areas of the leaves using a side-load float of Mix 4. When dry, deepen the under leaves and the triangle areas with Black Plum. Side-load float Cranberry Wine or Royal Purple accents on the outer edge leaves or the tips of all leaves. Side-load float a highlight in the center of the light area of the top leaves with a brush mix of Reindeer Moss Green + Titanium White. Add a side-load float of French Mauve to a few leaves for a tint of color. Side-load float highlights on the stroked petals with a lighter value of the first stroke.

- *Highlight the center rose strokes with Mix 1.*
- *Highlight the right rose strokes with French Mauve.*
- *Highlight the left rose strokes with French Mauve + Titanium White.*

Repeat the shade values on the roses to deepen the shade areas and to soften the strokes.

- *Shade the center rose with Antique Mauve.*
- *Shade the right rose with Cranberry Wine.*
- *Shade the left rose with Antique Mauve + Cranberry Wine.*

Side-load float in the throat and the base of the roses with a darker value.

- *Add a darker value to the center rose with Cranberry Wine.*
- *Add a darker value to the right rose with Black Plum.*
- *Add a darker value to the left rose with Cranberry Wine + Black Plum.*

Brush mix True Ochre + a touch of Black Plum and lighten with Mix 1. Load the mixture on a liner brush and dab the liner in the throat of the roses to create small pollen dots. Load Mix 3 on a ⅛-inch (3mm) angle and side load into Mix 1. Stroke in the filler flowers by setting the brush down, twisting and lifting off. Continue side loading into the light mixture and applying the petals. Some petals should be dark and some very light. When dry, side load a wash of Mix 2 and lightly side-load float where the flowers are under leaves or over any group of flowers that need to be deepened. Place a dot of Reindeer Moss Green in the center of the four-petal blossoms. Side-load float the small leaves with a thin side load of Mix 2 to deepen the shade areas. Load a liner brush with Light Avocado + a touch of Royal Purple and pull in tendrils throughout the design. Add strokes of Iridescent Gold Deep with a liner brush.

44 *Finishing the Stationery Box*

Using a 1-inch (25mm) wash brush, apply three coats of
J.W. etc. Right-Step Matte Varnish to finish your stationery box.
Your Victorian letter box is now ready to hold your love letters
and decorate your office desk. Roses are fun and, with practice, are easy to make.

Blue Violets
on a Porcelain Plate

Violets are delicate flowers that appeal to the feminine side of our nature. In addition to their namesake color, violets are available in soft pinks, whites and deep purples.

In this lesson we'll learn to create variety using different values of the same color. *The violets will be painted in a range of blue-violets, created by using different values of blue. The center of interest will have strong, dark values; as our eye moves away from that area, the blues become lighter and closer to the background color. The rusty red accents add a touch of complementary color for variety.*

Many floral designs incorporate ribbons, so I included one here to help you learn to create form through value placement and correct blending.

Color Mixes

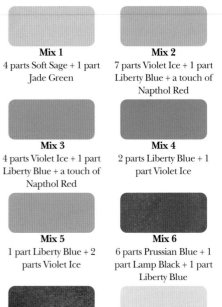

Mix 1
4 parts Soft Sage + 1 part Jade Green

Mix 2
7 parts Violet Ice + 1 part Liberty Blue + a touch of Napthol Red

Mix 3
4 parts Violet Ice + 1 part Liberty Blue + a touch of Napthol Red

Mix 4
2 parts Liberty Blue + 1 part Violet Ice

Mix 5
1 part Liberty Blue + 2 parts Violet Ice

Mix 6
6 parts Prussian Blue + 1 part Lamp Black + 1 part Liberty Blue

Mix 7
1 part Lamp Black + 6 parts Prussian Blue

Mix 8
1 part Silver Sage Green + 1 part Titanium White

Mix 9
4 parts Silver Sage Green + 1 part Midnite Green

Mix 10
Liberty Blue + a touch of Napthol Red

Mix 11
1 part Midnite Green + 1 part Hauser Medium Green

Mix 12
2 parts Napthol Red + 1 part Prussian Blue

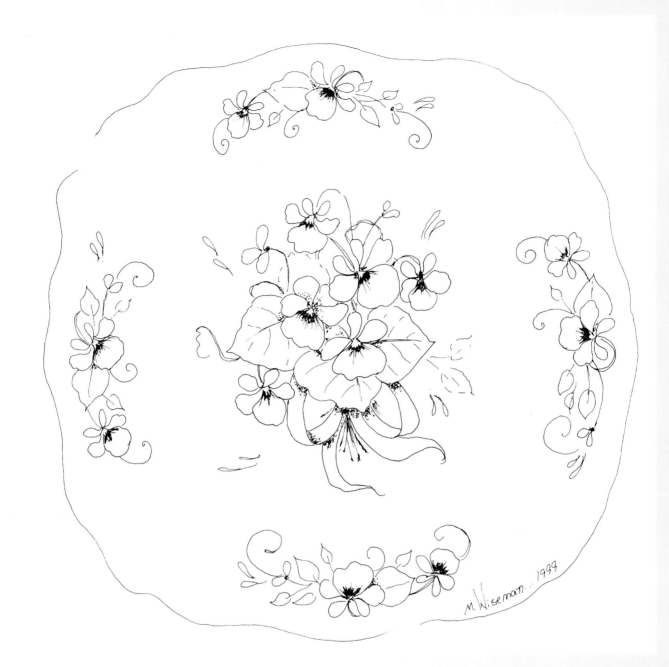

This pattern may be hand-traced or photocopied for personal use only. Enlarge at 154% on a photocopier to return to full size.

Materials

Surface

- This 9½" (24.1cm) diameter porcelain plate is available from Brenda Stewart by Design, 228 Yorkshire Dr., Williamsburg, VA 23185. Phone: (757) 564-7093.

DecoArt Americana Acrylic Paints

- Black Plum DA172
- Burnt Sienna DA63
- Hauser Medium Green DA132
- Jade Green DA57
- Lamp Black DA67
- Midnite Green DA84
- Napthol Red DA104
- Prussian Blue DA138
- Silver Sage Green DA149
- Soft Sage DA207
- Titanium White DA1
- True Ochre DA143

Delta Ceramcoat Acrylic Paints

- Liberty Blue 02416
- Violet Ice 02557

Brushes

- ¼-inch (6mm), ⅜-inch (10mm), ½-inch (12mm) and ¾-inch (19mm) angle brushes
- no. 10/0 liner
- no. 2 and no. 4 filberts

Additional Supplies

- tracing paper
- black or gray transfer paper
- wet palette or small paint pots
- Krylon Matte Finish Spray, no. 1311

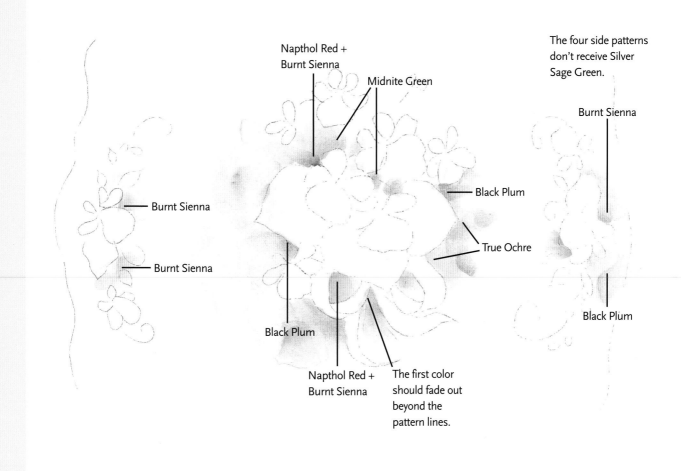

Napthol Red +
Burnt Sienna

Midnite Green

The four side patterns
don't receive Silver
Sage Green.

Burnt Sienna

Black Plum

Burnt Sienna

True Ochre

Burnt Sienna

Black Plum

Black Plum

Napthol Red +
Burnt Sienna

The first color
should fade out
beyond the
pattern lines.

1 Preparing the Surface and Creating the Background

Wash the porcelain plate in warm water with a mild liquid soap. Rinse in clear, warm water to remove any soap residue. Dry well with a lint-free towel. Transfer the design lines using black or gray transfer paper. With clear water, dampen the background behind the design lines and in any areas where the background shows between areas of the design. Allow the water to settle into the ground—it should disappear but the plate should feel damp. Side load a ¾-inch (19mm) angle brush or a brush that fits the area with Soft Sage thinned to a wash consistency. Side-load float this color into the background and allow the color to fade out beyond the design line. Place this color all the way around each of the four sides and the center floral design. When dry, side load thinned Silver Sage Green on a ½-inch (12mm) angle brush and deepen the triangle areas of the large center design. Also place in the shadow leaves at this time. Use clean water to thin Burnt Sienna, True Ochre, Napthol Red, Midnite Green and Black Plum and

pat tints into the areas marked. Other tints can be added to the background later, if desired. The plate has areas that are raised and recessed; slightly dampen these areas and wash thinned Silver Sage Green over them. Wipe with a soft cloth to remove the excess from the ridges and push the color into the recessed areas. Apply the color lightly and repeat the application.

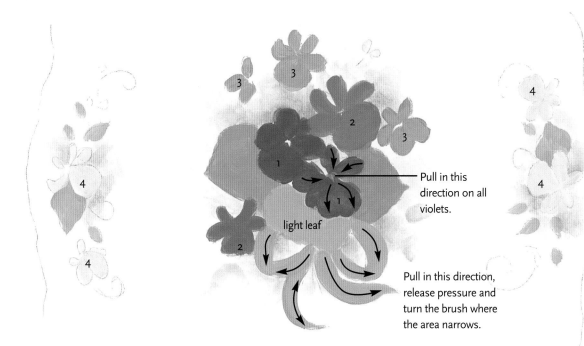

Pull in this
direction on all
violets.

light leaf

Pull in this direction,
release pressure and
turn the brush where
the area narrows.

2 Basecoating the Violets and Leaves

Using a fully loaded no. 2 or no. 4 filbert brush, block in the
violets with the appropriate colors listed below. The violets
may require more than one coat for opaque coverage.

- *Block in violets marked 1 with Liberty Blue.*
- *Block in violets marked 2 with Mix 5.*
- *Block in violets marked 3 with Mix 4.*
- *Block in violets marked 4 with Violet Ice.*

Using a fully loaded ⅜-inch (10mm) angle brush, block in the
light leaf using Mix 1 and the darker leaves with Jade Green.
Block in the leaves on the four border designs with a no. 2 filbert loaded with Silver Sage Green. Block in the ribbon with a
no. 4 filbert fully loaded with Mix 2. When blocking in the ribbons, pull in the direction indicated above.

X denotes light areas.

→ denotes direction of side-load float for shading.

3 Applying Shade Values to the Leaves, Light Values to the Violets and Shade Values to the Ribbon

Using a ½-inch (12mm) angle brush, side-load float Hauser Medium Green to shade all three leaves in the center. Shade the leaves on the four sides with a side-load float of Mix 9. On the leaves that have light on both outside edges, place the shade color in with a back-to-back float. To do this, place the long edge of the brush in the center next to the vein and pull toward the tip. Flip the brush over and shade on the other side of the vein. Shade the leaf that has a light near the vein area on the outside edge and fade in toward the vein area. Shade the other side of the leaf next to the vein and allow the color to fade toward the light area of the leaf. The color should fade over the light areas slightly. Side-load float in the light values on the violets with a ¼-inch (6mm) angle loaded with the colors listed at right. Place the light on each petal, following the areas marked with Xs. Apply more pressure to the brush where the area of the petal is wider and release the pressure and pull up on the brush where the area is narrow. Allow the application of color to dry, then apply the same color again.

• Float light values on the violets marked 1 with Mix 4.
• Float light values on the violets marked 2 with Mix 5.
• Float light values on the violets marked 3 with Violet Ice.
• Float light values on the violets marked 4 with Titanium White.

Using a ⅜-inch (10mm) brush, side-load float a Mix 3 shade on the ribbon. Pull the long edge of the brush across the top and bottom of each ribbon section, allowing the color to fade into the light areas on both sides. Side-load float the ribbon tails on one edge opposite the light side.

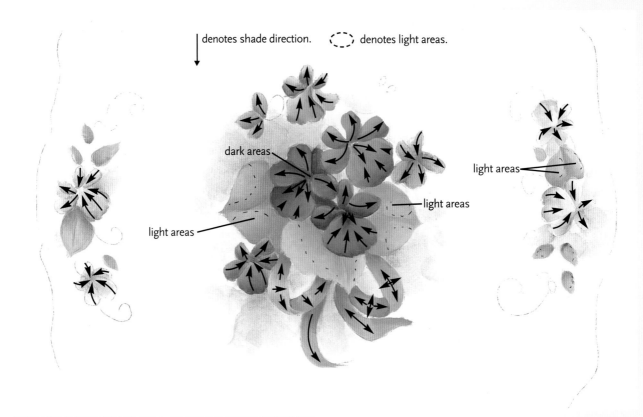

denotes shade direction.   denotes light areas.

dark areas

light areas

light areas

light areas

light areas

4 Applying Shade Values to the Violets and Light Values to the Leaves and Ribbons

Apply the shade values to each violet petal with a ⅜-inch (10mm) angle brush and a side-load float of the appropriate color listed below. Reload the brush after each application of color, except in small areas such as the back petals. Here you may paint one petal, flip the brush over and paint a second petal before reloading. Start on the back petals, then paint the side petals and last the center petals. It's best to pull in the directions indicated. Keep the long edge of the brush (with the most color) toward the area where more shading is required and the short side toward the area where the least color is desired. When applying side-load floated color to porcelain it's best to keep the brush on the dry side; otherwise the color will be difficult to control. The color may be applied twice for a smoother blend.

- *Shade the violets marked 1 with Mix 6.*
- *Shade the violets marked 2 with Liberty Blue.*
- *Shade the violets marked 3 with Mix 4.*
- *Shade the violets marked 4 with Mix 2.*

Using a ⅜-inch (10mm) angle brush, side load into the colors listed at right to apply the light values to the leaves. Place these light values on the outside edge, or near the vein lines and on the opposite side along the leaf edge. Lay the brush down in the center of the largest area, pull the color toward the base of the leaf and release the pressure as you pull. The color should fade away as the area gets tighter. Flip the brush over, lay it on the edge of the first placement and pull the brush toward the tip of the leaf. Again release the pressure on the brush as you pull. Place the long edge of the brush toward the leaf's edge or toward the vein line.

- *Lighten the light leaf with Soft Sage.*
- *Lighten the darker leaves with Mix 1.*
- *Apply the leaves on the four borders with Mix 8.*

When the first light is dry, apply a second light using the same color and applying it on top of the last color. Use a smaller brush or drybrush the second light on, keeping the color contained in the previous area. Apply the light value to the ribbon with a side-load float of Mix 2. Lighten with Violet Ice. Apply lights to the middle areas of each section of ribbon with a back-to-back float. To do this, place the long edge of the brush in the center and pull the brush across the width of the ribbon, allowing the color to fade up toward the top of the section. Flip the brush over, straddle the line and pull across the ribbon, letting the color fade toward the bottom of the section. Side-load float on one side of each tail to lighten the tails of the ribbon. When dry, repeat using Violet Ice. The second light should stay within the last application of color.

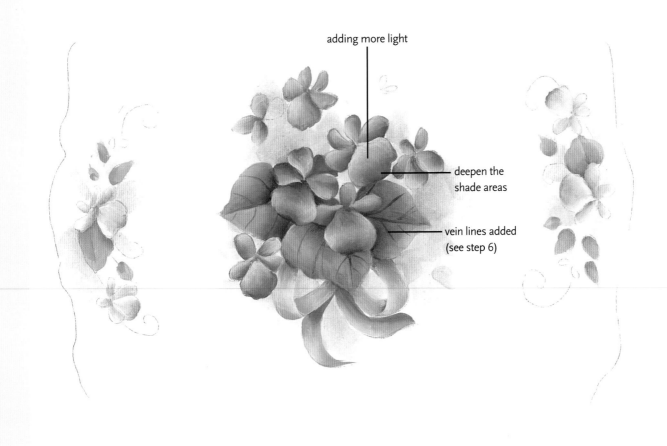

adding more light

deepen the
shade areas

vein lines added
(see step 6)

5 Building the Light and Dark Values on the Violets, Leaves and Ribbon

In this step, continue to build darks and lights with side-load floats of the colors listed below and at right. Drybrushing can be used when applying the light values. Choose a brush that fits each area. When applying the colors, stay within the last application of color each time another color is applied. It is helpful to use a smaller brush or load less color across the brush as the areas of application get tighter. Apply a darker shade value to the two darker leaves using Hauser Medium Green + a touch of Midnite Green. Repeat Hauser Medium Green on the lighter leaf. Apply the light values with a dry brush using Soft Sage on the darker leaves and Mix 8 on the lighter leaf. The leaves on the four sides are complete with only one light and shade applied.

- Deepen the violets marked 1 with Mix 7.
- Deepen the violets marked 2 with Mix 6.
- Deepen the violets marked 3 with Liberty Blue.

Lighten the light values on the violets using the following colors.

- Lighten the violets marked 1 with Mix 4 lightened with Violet Ice.
- Lighten the violets marked 2 with Violet Ice.
- Lighten the violets marked 3 with Violet Ice + Titanium White.

Deepen the ribbon with a side-load float of Mix 10 and lighten with a side-load float of Violet Ice + Titanium White.

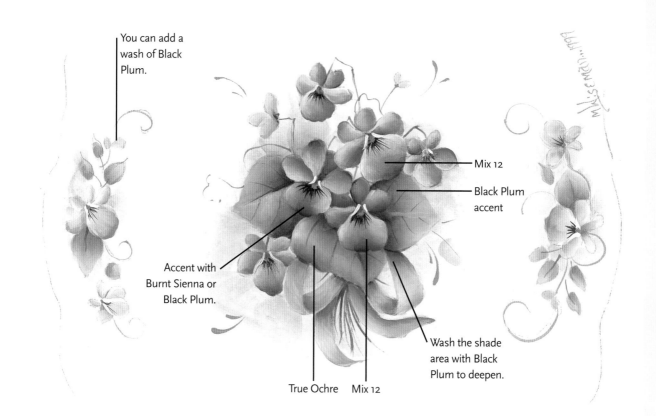

You can add a wash of Black Plum.

Accent with Burnt Sienna or Black Plum.

Mix 12

Black Plum accent

True Ochre

Mix 12

Wash the shade area with Black Plum to deepen.

6 Adding Final Darks, Highlights, Tints, Accents and Details

Using a 10/0 liner loaded with thinned Mix 11, line in the vein lines on the three leaves in the center. With a thin side-load float of Midnite Green, deepen the darkest area. Add accents to the shade areas with a side-load float of Burnt Sienna or Black Plum. Add highlights to the lightest areas of the leaves by drybrushing Titanium White with an old brush. The leaves can be warmed up with a very thin wash of True Ochre. Using a 10/0 liner loaded with Mix 11 thinned with water, stroke in all stems, veins and vines. Deepen the violets in the shade areas with thin side-load floats of Mix 7. Wash accent colors on some petal dark areas with Mix 12. Drybrush highlights in the light areas of violet 3 with Titanium White and on violets 1 and 2 with Violet Ice + Titanium White. Pull the background comma strokes with a 10/0 liner brush loaded with Mix 2.

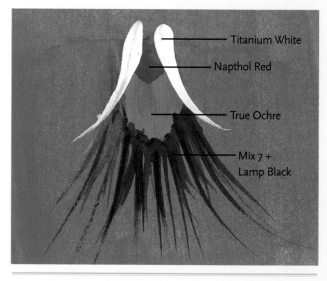

Titanium White

Napthol Red

True Ochre

Mix 7 + Lamp Black

7 Violet Centers and Beards

The large petal in each violet has a beard of very thin lines. Add Lamp Black to Mix 7 for violets 1 and 2. Use Mix 7 on violets 3 and 4. Thin these colors with water and pull down into the petal about two-thirds of the way toward the outside edge. Place a small press dot of True Ochre in the triangle area at the top of the large petal. When the True Ochre dot is dry, press in a Napthol Red dot at the top. Pull in a Titanium White comma stroke on each side of the True Ochre dot. The tail of the comma should pull into the petal edge.

8 Finishing the Project

Spray the piece with two or three light coats of Krylon Matte
Finish Spray, no. 1311. The plate is now ready to hang on a wall
to grace a special room in your home. If you enjoyed painting
this plate, try painting this design on a small box that has a
white background and share it with a friend.

Pink *Tulips*
on a Wooden Basket

Tulips have been cultivated for over five hundred years. Countless varieties display an amazing diversity of shapes and colors. This lesson focuses on the Clara Butt tulip—one of the Darwin tulips—with its soft pink flowers. The design is painted using a complementary red and green color scheme.

In this lesson we will learn to **paint a flower which is oval in shape when taken as a whole.** The form of each petal will be created by the placement of value and the blending direction.

The long, cylinder-shaped leaves beckon the artist to create the illusion of length and gracefulness, while really painting one section of the leaf at a time.

Color Mixes

Mix 1
1 part Titanium White +
1 part Cool Neutral

Mix 2
1 part Cool Neutral +
1 part Light Buttermilk

Mix 3
Mix 2 + a touch of
French Mauve

Mix 4
2 parts Mix 3 +
1 part French Mauve

Mix 5
2 parts French Mauve +
1 part Mauve

Mix 6
2 parts Mauve + 1 part
French Mauve

Mix 7
1 part Mix 2 +
1 part Mauve

Mix 8
1 part Mix 6 +
1 part Antique Mauve

Mix 9
1 part Mix 8 + a touch of
Midnite Green

Mix 10
1 part Mix 7 +
1 part Mix 2

Mix 11
1 part Antique Mauve +
1 part Mix 9

Mix 12
1 part Antique Mauve +
1 part Cranberry Wine

Mix 13
1 part Reindeer Moss
Green + 1 part Light
Buttermilk

Mix 14
1 part Cranberry Wine +
1 part Black Plum

This pattern may be hand-traced or photocopied for personal use only. Enlarge at 143% on a photocopier to return to full size.

M. Wiseman...1999

Materials

Surface
- This 10½" × 6¾" × 11" (26.7cm × 17.2cm × 27.9cm) basket (#43B) is available from The Pop Shop, Norman & Simone Guillemette, RR 2 Box 1524, New Dam Rd., Sanford, ME 04073. Phone: (207) 324-5946. Web site: www.cybertours.com/~popshop/pophome.htm

DecoArt Americana Acrylic Paints
- Antique Mauve DA162
- Black Plum DA172
- Blue/Grey Mist DA105
- Celery Green DA208
- Cool Neutral DA89
- Cranberry Wine DA112
- French Mauve DA186
- Light Avocado DA106
- Light Buttermilk DA164
- Mauve DA26
- Midnite Green DA84
- Moon Yellow DA7
- Plantation Pine DA113
- Reindeer Moss Green DA187
- Shale Green DA152
- Titanium White DA1
- True Ochre DA143

Brushes
- ¼-inch (6mm), ⅜-inch (10mm), ½-inch (12mm) and ¾-inch (19mm) angle brushes
- no. 6 fabric round or spatter tool
- no. 2 and no. 6 round brushes
- no. 10/0 liner
- polyfoam brush
- 1-inch (25mm) wash brush

Additional Supplies
- 320-grit wet /dry sandpaper
- J.W. etc. Right-Step Matte Varnish
- Designs From the Heart Wood Sealer
- tracing paper
- black or gray transfer paper
- wet palette or small paints pots

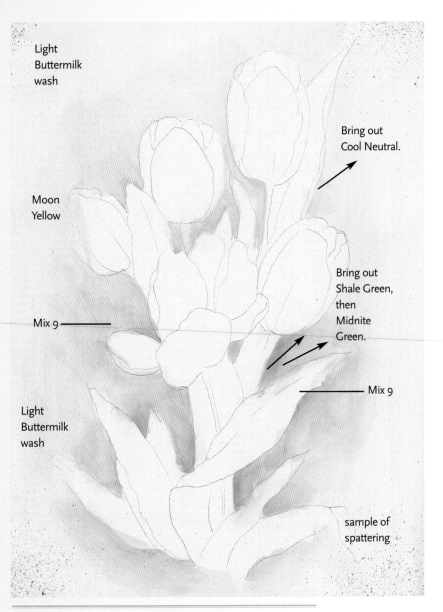

Light
Buttermilk
wash

Bring out
Cool Neutral.

Moon
Yellow

Bring out
Shale Green,
then
Midnite
Green.

Mix 9

Mix 9

Light
Buttermilk
wash

sample of
spattering

1 *Preparing the Surface and Creating the Background*

Seal the entire basket inside and out using Designs From the Heart Wood Sealer. When the sealer is dry, sand the basket using 320-grit sandpaper. Using a tack rag, wipe off the sanding dust. Basecoat the front and back panels with Mix 1 and a polyfoam brush. Apply two to three coats for opaque coverage, sanding lightly between coats. Basecoat the three panels on each side of the basket, the rim and the interior of the basket with Shale Green loaded on a polyfoam brush. Apply as many coats as needed for opaque coverage, sanding between coats. Transfer the design lines using black or gray transfer paper. Place the leaves right on the bottom edge of the basket. With clear water, dampen the background behind the design lines and in any areas where the background shows between areas of the design. Allow the water to settle into the ground—it should disappear but the wood should feel damp.

Side load a ¾-inch (19mm) angle brush or a brush that fits the area with Cool Neutral thinned to a wash consistency. Side-load float this color into the background and allow the color to fade out as far as the design line. When dry, side load thinned Shale Green on a ¾-inch (19mm) angle brush and deepen the triangle areas of the design. Side-load float Shale Green under the basket rim, down each of the sides and across the basket bottom; the color should fade in toward the design. Thin Moon Yellow, Mix 7, Light Buttermilk and Midnite Green with water and wash these tints into the areas marked. Other tints can be added to the background later, if desired. Brush mix a small amount of Midnite Green into Shale Green and thin with water to an ink-like consistency. Load a no. 6 fabric brush with this mixture and lightly spatter the four corners of the basket. When dry, repeat using Mix 9.

Two washes of Cool Neutral have been applied to this side.

One wash of Mix 1 has been applied to this side and spattering has been added on top.

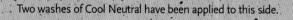

2 Painting the Basket

Wash over the Shale Green areas of the basket with Cool Neutral thinned with water, using a 1-inch (25mm) rake brush. Start under the top band and streak each Shale Green section. Allow to dry, then apply Mix 1 in the same manner except use less of this color. Allow to dry. Spatter the Shale Green areas with Midnite Green thinned with water and a no. 6 fabric brush. Repeat with Cranberry Wine.

flip area

stem

3 Basecoating the Tulips and Leaves

- Using a no. 6 round brush fully loaded with Celery Green, block in the leaves that aren't numbered.
- Wash the leaf marked 1 with Reindeer Moss Green, using a no. 6 round brush.
- Block in the leaves marked 2 with Light Avocado.
- Block in the leaves marked 3 with a wash of Shale Green.
- Block in the flipped areas of all stems and leaves with Reindeer Moss Green, using a no. 2 round brush.

Using a fully loaded no. 6 round brush, block in the tulips with the appropriate color listed below and at right. Block each tulip in as a whole rather than petal by petal. Apply the pattern when the base colors are dry. The tulips and leaves will require more then one coat for opaque coverage.

- Block in tulip 1 with Mix 3.
- Block in tulip 2 with Mix 4.
- Block in tulip 3 with Mix 5.
- Block in tulip 4 with Mix 6.
- Block in tulip 5 with Mix 7.

Hint

You can block in areas quickly and create fewer ridges by using a round brush. When loading the brush, flatten the brush hairs. Load one side by pulling through the paint, then turn the brush over and load the other side. The paint should completely fill the hairs of the brush right up to the ferrule. Start inside the area to be blocked in and pull in a vertical stroke with pressure on the hairs. If the area gets narrow, pull up on the brush hairs.

start here

lighten here

start brush here

4 Applying the First Shade Values to the Tulips and the Light Values to the Leaves

Using a ½-inch (12mm) angle brush, side-load float Reindeer Moss Green on the light areas of the unnumbered leaves. Paint each leaf as a section rather than as a whole. Lay the brush down in the largest area first and pull down, then flip the brush over and pull in the other direction. The light area is on one side of the vein line and fades toward the outside edge. Lighten the other side of the leaf on the outside edge and fade in toward the vein area. The color should blend out further in the center area and less as the object gets narrow. Allow the colors to dry, then reapply the same colors for better coverage.

- *Lighten the leaves marked 1 with Light Buttermilk.*
- *Lighten the leaves marked 2 with Celery Green.*
- *No light is applied to the leaves marked 3.*

Apply the first shade value to each of the tulips using a ½-inch (12mm) angle brush and a side-load float of the appropriate color listed below. Place the edge of the brush with the strong color in the darkest area and then fade away. Apply in the direction indicated. In some cases the shade will be applied on both sides of a line; it will be separated later by applying more shade color to one of the areas.

- *Shade the tulip marked 1 with Mix 4. Float on the left side with Celery Green.*
- *Shade the tulip marked 2 with Mix 4.*
- *Shade the tulip marked 3 with Mix 5.*
- *Shade the tulip marked 4 with Mix 8.*
- *Shade the tulip marked 5 with Mix 9.*

5 Applying Light Value to the Tulips and Shade Values to the Leaves

Using a ½-inch (12mm) angle brush, side-load float a shade of Light Avocado on all leaves. Shade the section of leaf that has a light near the vein area on the outside edge and fade in toward the vein area. Shade the other side of the leaf next to the vein and side-load float toward the outer edge of light. This color should fade over the light areas slightly. Follow the brush directions marked. Side-load float the light values in with a ½-inch (12mm) angle loaded with the appropriate light value for each tulip. Place the light on each petal, following the areas marked with Xs. Apply more pressure to the brush where the

area of the petal is wider and release the pressure and pull up on the brush where the area is narrow. Allow the application of color to dry and apply the same color again.

- *The light value for tulip 1 is Mix 2.*
- *The light value for tulip 2 is Mix 3.*
- *The light value for tulip 3 is Mix 4.*
- *The light value for tulip 4 is Mix 7.*
- *The light value for tulip 5 is Mix 10.*

second shade here ——— no second shade

no second shade

6 Building the Light and Dark Values on the Tulips and Leaves

In this step, continue to build darks and lights with side-load floats. Drybrushing can be used when applying the light values. Choose a brush that fits each area. When applying the colors, stay within the last application of color each time another color is applied. It's helpful to use a smaller brush or load less color across the brush as the areas of application get tighter. Apply a darker shade value to the tulips using the following colors.

- *Use Mix 3 on tulip 1, even over the Celery Green areas. Repeat.*
- *Use Mix 8 on tulip 2. Repeat.*
- *Use Mix 8 on tulip 3. Repeat using Antique Mauve.*
- *Use Mix 11 on tulip 4. Repeat using Mix 12.*
- *Use very thin Mix 11 on tulip 5. Repeat using Mix 11.*

Lighten the light values on the tulips using the following colors.

- *Lighten tulip 1 with Mix 2 + Light Buttermilk.*
- *Lighten tulip 2 with Mix 2.*
- *Lighten tulip 3 with Mix 3.*
- *Lighten tulip 4 with Mix 10.*
- *Lighten tulip 5 with Mix 3.*

Deepen the Celery-colored leaves (leaf 1) with a second side-load float of Light Avocado. When dry, repeat using Plantation Pine. Deepen leaf 2 with Plantation Pine. Apply thin side-load floats of Midnite Green to the leaves marked 3. Lighten the light values on the Celery-colored leaves with Mix 13. Use Reindeer Moss Green on leaf 2. Wash over the leaves marked 3 with Blue/Grey Mist thinned with water. Use Mix 2 on leaf 1.

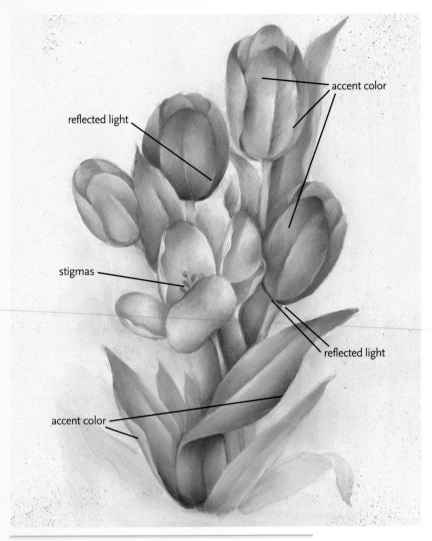

reflected light

accent color

stigmas

reflected light

accent color

7 Adding Final Darks, Highlights, Tints, Accents and Details

Apply the dark values with side-load floats, staying within the last application of color.

- *Use very thin Antique Mauve on tulip 1. The green areas can have a very thin application of Light Avocado.*
- *Use Mix 12 on tulip 2 and 3.*
- *Use Mix 14 on tulip 4.*
- *Further shading is required on tulip 5.*

Lighten the light values on the tulips by drybrushing or side-load floating on the following colors.

- *Use Light Buttermilk on tulip 1.*
- *Use Mix 2 + Light Buttermilk on tulip 2.*
- *Use Mix 2 on tulip 3.*
- *Use Mix 7 on tulip 4; if a lighter value is needed, use a brush mix of Mix 3 and Mix 7.*
- *Use Mix 2 on tulip 5.*

Apply reflected light to the areas marked using a side-load float of Blue/Grey Mist. Apply accent washes of Celery Green or Light Avocado with a side-load float in the areas marked. The leaves can be deepened with a side-load float of Midnite Green, or Plantation Pine can be repeated. Add accent side-load floats of Cranberry Wine to some of the leaves in the darkest areas. Drybrush or side-load float highlights on the Celery Green leaves using Mix 13 lightened with Light Buttermilk. The unmarked leaves don't receive a highlight. Lighten the centers of the stems with a side-load float of Mix 13. Shade the stems with a thin side-load float of Light Avocado, then glaze over the green with Cranberry Wine. Lighten the flip area of the leaves with Mix 13 and side-load float along the outside edges with Light Avocado. Press the stigmas in with a no. 2 round loaded with True Ochre + Black Plum. When dry, wash a small amount of Moon Yellow over the tip of each press dot. Using a 1-inch (25mm) wash brush, apply three coats of J.W. etc. Right-Step Matte Varnish to finish the basket. Your basket can be used to hold magazines or for a wastepaper basket in your favorite room.

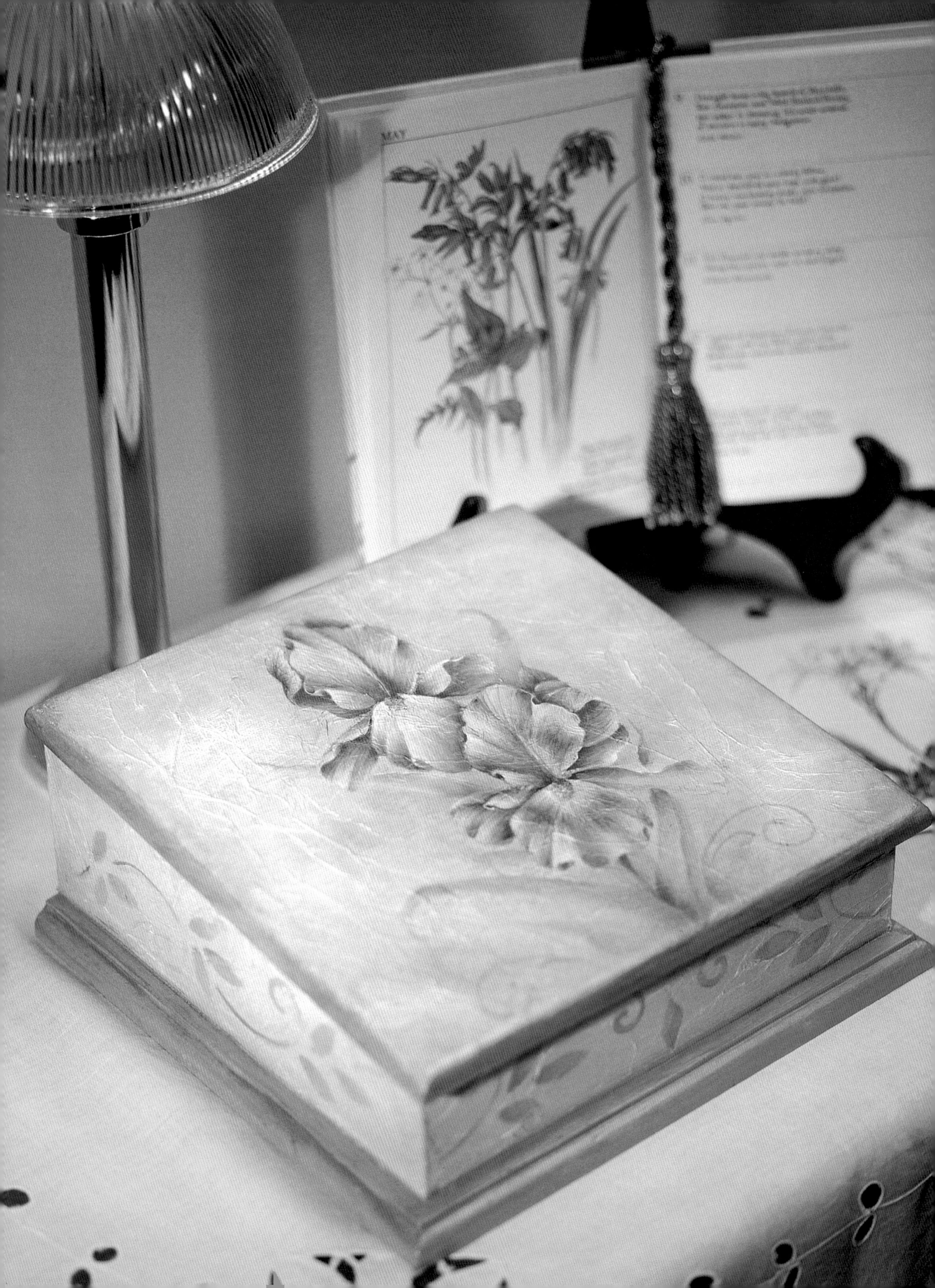

Two Irises

on a Slant-Top Box

The iris is a very graceful flower that reminds me of the Victorian times. In this lesson you will learn to **paint the folds and tucks that create the ruffled appearance of the iris;** you'll also learn the importance of stroke direction. The background is created by applying tissue paper over a gray-green basecoat. This adds an appearance of translucency and age to the design. I've painted this design on a slant-top box; this design would also be suitable for a framed canvas. The border design is stenciled on and then shaded.

Color Mixes

Mix 1
1 part Violet Ice + 1 part
Deep Periwinkle

Mix 2
2 parts Ultra Blue Deep
+ 3 parts Royal Plum + 1
part Deep Periwinkle

Mix 3
2 parts Ultra Blue Deep
+ 3 parts Royal Plum

Mix 4
1 part Titanium White +
1 part Orchid

Mix 5
1 part Titanium White +
2 parts Ultra Blue Deep

Mix 6
2 parts Dark Goldenrod
+ 1 part Black Plum

Mix 7
3 parts Earth Brown + 1
part Hunter Green

This pattern may be hand-traced or photocopied for personal use only. Enlarge at 143% on a photocopier to return to full size.

Materials

Surface

- This 9" × 9" (22.9cm × 22.9cm) slant-top box is available from Allen Wood Crafts, 3020 Dogwood Lane, Rt. 3, Supulpa, OK 74066. Phone: (918) 224-8796; Fax: (918) 224-3208.

DecoArt Americana Acrylic Paints

- Black Plum DA172
- Cool Neutral DA89
- Deep Periwinkle DA212
- Jade Green DA57
- Light Avocado DA106
- Lilac DA32
- Marigold DA194
- Orchid DA33
- Plum DA175
- Shale Green DA152
- Titanium White DA1
- Ultra Blue Deep DA100

DecoArt Heavenly Hues

- Celestial Blue DHH29
- Earth Brown DHH6
- Golden Halo DHH16
- Hunter Green DHH14
- Meadow Green DHH28
- Purple Heather DHH25
- White Cloud DHH1

Plaid Decorator Glaze

- New Gold Leaf 53002

Delta Ceramcoat

- Dark Goldenrod 02519
- Royal Plum 02560
- Violet Ice 02557

Brushes

- Langnickel series 5005, no. 6 round
- no. 6 round
- ⅛-inch (3mm), ¼-inch (6mm), ⅜-inch (10mm), ½-inch (12mm), ⅝-inch (15mm) and ¾-inch (19mm) angle brushes
- no. 10/0 liner
- 1-inch (25mm) wash brush
- 1-inch (25mm) polyfoam brush

Additional Supplies

- scraps of T-shirt material
- 320-grit wet/dry sandpaper
- J.W. etc. Right-Step Matte Varnish
- Designs From the Heart Wood Sealer
- Jo Sonja All Purpose Sealer
- one sheet of white tissue paper (the gift-wrap type)
- tracing paper
- black or gray transfer paper
- white transfer paper
- waxed palette paper
- Plaid Simply Stencils Scrolling Vine, no. 28172

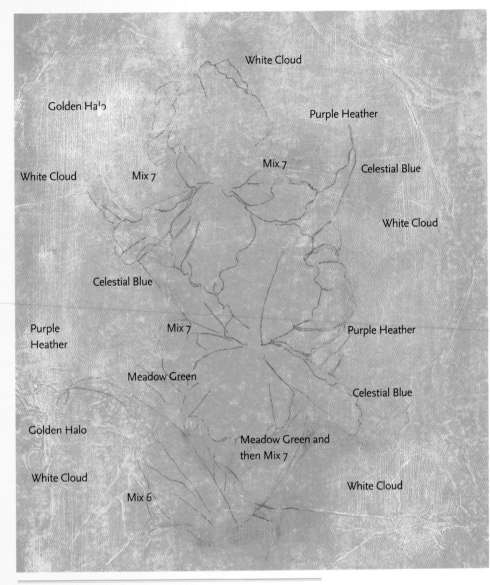

White Cloud

Golden Halo

Purple Heather

White Cloud   Mix 7

Mix 7

Celestial Blue

White Cloud

Celestial Blue

Purple
Heather   Mix 7

Purple Heather

Meadow Green

Celestial Blue

Golden Halo

Meadow Green and
then Mix 7

White Cloud

White Cloud

Mix 6

1 *Preparing the Surface and Creating the Background*

Seal the entire box with Designs From the Heart Wood Sealer. When the sealer is dry, sand the wood using 320-grit sandpaper. Using a tack rag, wipe off the sanding dust. Basecoat the lid and the bottom edge of the box with Shale Green on a dry polyfoam brush. Basecoat the back and three sides with a polyfoam brush and Cool Neutral. Apply as many coats as needed for opaque coverage, sanding lightly between coats. Cut five pieces of tissue paper slightly larger than the area each is to cover. You'll need one for each of the three sides, one for the lid and one for the back. Apply one coat of Jo Sonja All Purpose Sealer to the sides and back of the box using a polyfoam brush. Lay a piece of the tissue on top of the wet sealer and press the paper down with your fingertips. Allow the paper to wrinkle as you press it onto the surface. Cover all three sides and the back of the box in this manner. Apply another coat of sealer over the tissue before it dries. Cover the lid last; the tissue should stop just before the edge of the lid starts to roll over. Allow the sealer to dry thoroughly. Transfer the pattern for the iris and leaves with black transfer paper. Squeeze a quarter-size puddle of each of the Heavenly Hues colors onto your waxed palette paper. Dip a soft, 1-inch (25cm) square of T-shirt fabric into the color that is to be applied and rub it into the area marked. Start rubbing close to the design lines and fade the color as you move away. The colors should blend into each other where they meet. Allow the colors to dry, then reapply if desired. Rub the areas closest to the leaves with Meadow Green, then with Mix 7. The more you rub the colors into the background, the softer they will appear. You may apply the tight areas with a brush to avoid erasing the pattern lines. It's important that you place the White Cloud areas exactly as shown; these areas represent light striking the design. The other tints can be placed in the general areas marked.

red-violet iris

blue-violet iris

2 Basecoating the Irises and Leaves

Using a ⅝-inch (15mm) angle brush fully loaded with Deep Periwinkle, basecoat the entire blue-violet iris. Block in the red-violet iris with Orchid. When dry, apply as many coats as needed to each flower to achieve solid coverage. Using a no. 6 round brush loaded with Jade Green, block in all of the leaves. When dry, apply a second coat. (See the hint on page 81 for blocking in areas with a round brush.) Transfer the petal lines onto the irises using white transfer paper.

3 Applying the Light Values to the Irises and Leaves

Apply the light values to the irises using a ½-inch (12mm) angle brush and a side-load float of Mix 1 on the blue-violet iris and Lilac on the red-violet iris. Apply the color to one petal at a time. On petals that fold over, it's best to paint each section individually. Pull the color across the area of the petal, wipe the brush on a paper towel and sweep the color in toward the vein area. Apply lights to the middle of the petals where needed with a back-to-back float. When applying the vein lines, side

load the brush, then stand it on the chisel edge with the long corner of the brush at the bottom of the vein. Sweep off toward the vein tip, releasing the pressure as you pull. Repeat these colors, if desired. Follow the arrows for stroke direction. Using a ½-inch (12mm) angle brush, side-load float Cool Neutral light values on each leaf in the areas indicated. Repeat for better coverage.

4 Adding Shading to the Irises and Leaves

Apply the shade colors using side-load floats of Mix 2 on the blue-violet iris, Plum on the red-violet iris and Light Avocado on the leaves. Lay the brush on the surface with the dark side toward the dark area. Shade one petal or section at a time, following the direction indicated above. Allow these colors to value over toward the light areas; they may even float slightly into the light areas. Keep the first side-load float broad enough that other shade values can be applied in the same area. Skizzle the color in as you side-load float, allowing lines of shading to appear.

5 Continue to Strengthen the Shade and Light Values on the Irises and Leaves

Using an angle brush that fits the area where the color is to be applied, strengthen the light and dark values with the colors listed below; these colors will build on the last color applied. Use the same stroke direction and method of application as in step four. Apply the light value first.

- *Lighten the blue-violet iris with Violet Ice.*
- *Lighten the red-violet iris with Mix 4.*
- *Lighten the leaves with Cool Neutral brush mixed with a touch of Titanium White.*

When these colors are dry, apply the dark values.

- *Darken the blue-violet iris with Mix 3.*
- *Darken the red-violet iris with Royal Plum.*
- *Darken the leaves with Light Avocado.*

Repeat all lights and darks when dry, applying the colors in the same order as before. Keep the second application within the previous layer.

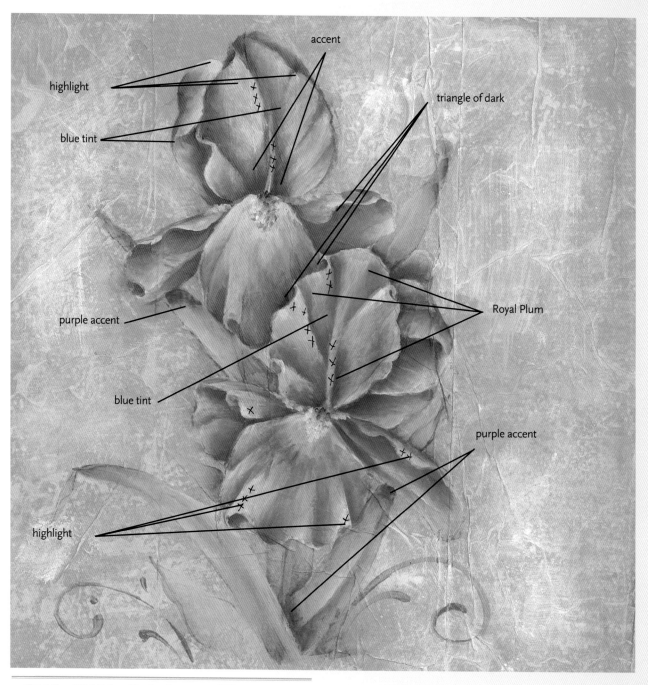

highlight

accent

blue tint

triangle of dark

purple accent

Royal Plum

blue tint

purple accent

highlight

6 Adding Highlights, Darks, Accents and Tints to the Irises and Leaves

Side-load float the darkest value into the triangle areas of the flower petals. Use Mix 3 on the blue-violet iris and Black Plum on the red-violet iris. Side load a slightly damp ¼-inch (6mm) angle brush with Titanium White and drag it over the lightest areas (the areas that protrude most) on both irises to create a highlight. Add a blue tint to the irises by washing over the middle values with Mix 5. Wash an accent of Mix 3 on the dark areas of the red-violet iris. Wash an accent of Royal Plum on the dark areas of the blue-violet iris. Using a ½-inch (12mm) angle brush, side-load float an accent of Mix 3 over the dark areas of the leaves. When dry, wash a glaze over the bottom of

the leaves with New Gold Leaf. Side load a ¾-inch (19mm) angle brush with New Gold Leaf and side-load float around the outer edges of the lid, allowing the color to fade in toward the design. Continue to side-load float New Gold Leaf into the triangular areas of the background between the leaves and flowers. Wash over the outer edge of the box lid and the lower routed bottom of the box with New Gold Leaf. Repeat several times, allowing each application to dry before applying another. Using a 10/0 liner loaded with New Gold Leaf thinned slightly with water, apply the strokework on both sides of the design.

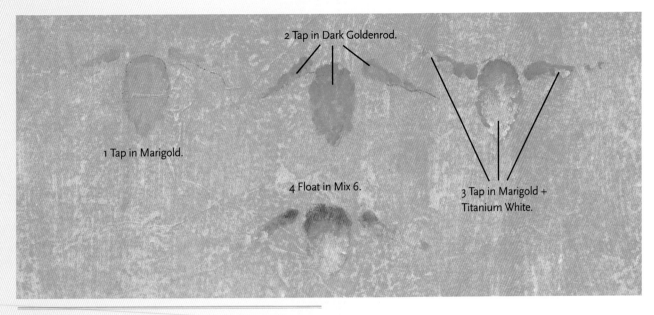

2 Tap in Dark Goldenrod.

1 Tap in Marigold.

4 Float in Mix 6.

3 Tap in Marigold + Titanium White.

7 *Painting the Iris Beards*

Side load a dry ⅛-inch (3mm) angle brush with Marigold and tap in the beard areas. Use only the long corner of the brush to tap into the area. While this color is wet, tap Dark Goldenrod into the corner areas and into the top third of the larger beard. Wipe the brush and side load with Marigold,

then touch into Titanium White. Blend the colors together on your palette and tap into the outer areas of the beard on the side and in the lower third of the center beard. When dry, side-load float a shade on the inside corners of both side beards and at the top edge of the center beard with Mix 6.

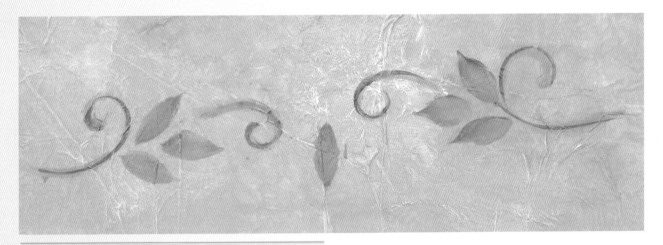

8 *Finishing the Box*

Stencil the border design on using a soft Langnickel no. 6 round tipped into Shale Green (see page 17). Work the color into the brush well. Using a circular motion, apply the color to the open areas of the stencil. Lift and move the stencil to repeat the design. Start near the center and move along toward the back of the box, then flip the stencil over and repeat the design on the other side of the box. Reload the brush each time you complete a leaf and stem. Do not clean the brush or add water to it until the stenciling is complete. Allow the border de-

sign to dry, then use a ½-inch (12mm) angle brush to side-load float New Gold Leaf on the base and tip of each leaf. Outline the stem with a liner brush loaded with New Gold Leaf. Using a 1-inch (25mm) wash brush, finish with several coats of J.W. etc. Right-Step Matte Varnish. The box is now finished and ready to be placed in your favorite room. It adds a nice touch to a dresser or bath area to hold small treasures, or in the office to hold your special stationery.

White Poinsettias
on a Candle Coaster

The poinsettia is one of my favorite flowers to paint and decorate with in the winter months. The poinsettia is different from many of the other flowers because its "petals" are really leaves. Traditionally this plant is red, but it can be painted in many hues, such as the white poinsettia in this lesson. Because the background is gray-green, I shaded the poinsettia with grayed-down green values. This color choice creates a warm, yet soft, holiday spirit. In this lesson we will continue to use the same blending methods learned in previous projects. The focus of this lesson will be on **painting a white flower.**

Color Mixes

Mix 1
2 parts Raw Sienna + 1 part Plantation Pine

Mix 2
2 parts Asphaltum + 1 part Plantation Pine

Mix 3
2 parts Napthol Red + 1 part Plantation Pine

Mix 4
1 part Buttermilk + 1 part Yellow Ochre

Mix 5
2 parts Napthol Red + 1 part Yellow Ochre

This pattern may be hand-traced or photocopied for personal use only. Enlarge at 145% on a photocopier to return to full size.

Materials

Surface

- This 10-inch (25.4cm) diameter round, turned candle/wine coaster (WD1306) is available from the Stonebridge Collection, 4411 Bee Ridge Rd., Suite 256, Sarasota, FL 34233. Phone: (800) ART TOLE.

DecoArt Americana Acrylic Paints

- Asphaltum DA180
- Black Plum DA172
- Buttermilk DA3
- Jade Green DA57
- Light Avocado DA106
- Light Buttermilk DA164
- Napthol Red DA104
- Plantation Pine DA113
- Reindeer Moss Green DA187
- Shale Green DA152
- Yellow Ochre DA8

Delta Ceramcoat Acrylic Paint

- Raw Sienna 023411

Plaid Decorator Glaze

- Olde World Bronze 53004

Brushes

- ⅛-inch (3mm), ¼-inch (6mm), ⅜-inch (10mm), ½-inch (12mm) and ⅝-inch

(15mm) angle brushes
- no. 10/0 liner
- no. 6 fabric round or spatter tool
- no. 2 and no. 6 rounds
- no. 6 flat
- 1-inch (25mm) polyfoam brush
- 1-inch (25mm) wash brush

Additional Supplies

- 320-grit wet/dry sandpaper
- tack rag
- J.W. etc. Right-Step Matte Varnish
- Designs From the Heart Wood Sealer
- tracing paper
- white transfer paper
- waxed palette paper

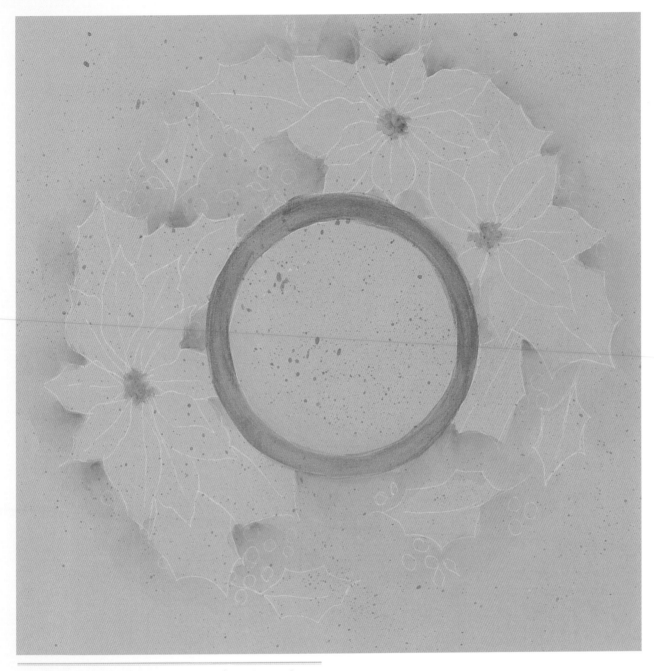

1 *Preparing the Surface and Creating the Background*

Seal the entire coaster and candle cup with Designs From the Heart Wood Sealer. When the sealer is dry, sand the wood using 320-grit sandpaper. Using a tack rag, wipe off the sanding dust. Basecoat the coaster and candle cup with Shale Green using a polyfoam brush. Apply as many coats as needed for opaque coverage, sanding lightly between coats. Transfer the design lines using white transfer paper. Dampen the background behind the design lines and in any areas where the background shows between areas of the design with clear water. Allow the water to settle into the ground—it should disappear but the wood should feel damp. Side load a ⅝-inch (15mm) angle brush or a brush that fits the area with

Mix 1 thinned to a wash consistency. Side-load float the color into the background and allow it to fade out as far as the design line. When dry, side load thinned Plantation Pine on a ½-inch (12mm) angle brush and deepen the triangle areas of the design. Next apply Black Plum in the triangular areas, then a wash of Olde World Bronze. Load a no. 6 fabric round brush with Olde World Bronze thinned with water to an ink-like consistency and lightly spatter the entire coaster and candle cup. Load Olde World Bronze on a no. 6 flat brush and base in the upper and lower rim. The trim may need more then one coat for solid coverage.

2 *Basecoating the Poinsettia Petals, Leaves and Berries*

Load a no. 6 round with Buttermilk thinned slightly with water and basecoat the flower petals. Block in the petals in the back first and the ones on top last. When dry, apply one more coat to each petal. The background will still show through the basecoat slightly. Block the berries in with Buttermilk on a no. 6 round brush. Load a ½-inch (12mm) angle brush with Jade Green and block in all the leaves marked 1. Use Reindeer Moss Green on the leaves marked 2. Load a no. 6 round brush with Reindeer Moss Green and block in all the small leaves near the berries. The larger leaves will require more than one coat for opaque coverage.

3 Applying the First Shade Value to the Poinsettia Petals, Berries and Leaves

Using a ½-inch (12mm) angle brush, side-load float Light Avocado on the leaves marked 1. Lay the brush down at the base of the leaf and pull toward the tip. Shade some of the leaves on one side of the vein and fade the color toward the outside of the leaf. Shade the other side of the leaf on the outside edge and fade in toward the vein line. Follow the stroke directions indicated above. Allow the color to dry, then repeat with Light Avocado. Shade the leaves marked 2 using Jade Green and repeat with a thin float of Light Avocado. Using a ⅜-inch (10mm) angle brush, side-load float Yellow Ochre shading on all of the poinsettia petals, starting with the back petals and finishing with the top petals. Pull the brush in the direction indicated, staying up on the brush edge in tight areas and laying the brush flat in wide areas. The petals of the poinsettia are really leaves, so paint them using the same technique you used to paint the leaves. The leaves contain a center vein line; apply the shading on one side of the vein or on both sides. The color should value out toward the outer edges of the leaf or fade in toward the vein area. Shade the berries on one side with a side-load float of Yellow Ochre. When dry, repeat the shading on the petals and berries with more Yellow Ochre.

4 Applying the Light Values to the Poinsettia Petals, Leaves and Berries

Using a ½-inch (12mm) angle brush, side-load float Reindeer Moss Green on the leaves marked 1 and Buttermilk on the leaves marked 2. Lay the brush down in the largest area first and pull down, then flip the brush over and pull in the other direction. The color should blend out further in the center area and less as the object gets narrow. The areas of light are indicated with Xs. Allow the colors to dry, then reapply for better coverage. Side-load float the light values in with a ¼-inch (6mm) angle side loaded with Buttermilk. Place the light on each petal in the areas marked with Xs. Apply more pressure to the brush where the area of the petal is wider and release the pressure and pull up on the brush where the area is narrow. Allow the application of color to dry, then reapply to deepen. Side-load float a Buttermilk light value in the areas marked with Xs on each berry, using a ⅛-inch (3mm) angle brush.

5 Building the Light and Dark Values on the Poinsettia Petals, Leaves and Berries and Placing in the Flower Centers

In this step, continue to build darks and lights with side-load floats. Choose a brush that fits each area. When applying the colors, stay within the last application of color each time another color is applied. It's helpful to use a smaller brush or load less color across the brush as the areas of application get tighter. Add a lighter value to the leaves marked 1 with Buttermilk brush mixed with Reindeer Moss Green. Lighten the leaves marked 2 with Buttermilk brush mixed with Light Buttermilk. Deepen the shade areas on all leaves with Plantation Pine. Darken the poinsettia petals with side-load floats of Mix 1. Apply a second dark with a thin side-load float of Plantation Pine. Lighten the light areas with a side-load float of Buttermilk. Side-load float Mix 1 on the shaded side of each berry. When dry, apply a thin side-load float on top of the last shade with Mix 3. Using a no. 2 round, place small dots in the center areas of the plants with Mix 5.

accent   tint   tint   accent

tint

tint

tint

tint

accent

accent

tint

accent   tint

tint

accent

6 Adding Final Darks, Highlights, Tints, Accents and Details

Using a 10/0 liner loaded with thinned Reindeer Moss Green lightened with Buttermilk, pull the center vein lines and the extending side vein lines. Deepen the leaves marked 1 with Mix 2, then add very thin Black Plum accents in the shade areas. Side-load float tints of Raw Sienna and Mix 3 or 5 in the middle areas using a ¼-inch (6mm) angle brush. Side-load float highlights on the leaves marked 1 with Buttermilk lightened with Light Buttermilk and on leaves marked 2 with Light Buttermilk. Deepen the petals with Black Plum. Add tints to the petals with thin side-load floats of Napthol Red in the dark areas and Mix 4 in the mid-value areas. Side-load float highlights on the petals with Light Buttermilk. Line the center veins

with Buttermilk. Lighten the veins on the top petals with Light Buttermilk. Lighten the center dots with a side-load float of Buttermilk loaded on an ⅛-inch (3mm) angle brush. Side-load float the shading on the top with Mix 3. Load a 10/0 liner brush with Mix 1 thinned with water and pull stems to the berries and leaves. Pull the tendrils that weave in and out of the design with Mix 1. Some of the berries should have dots at the bottom with small "hairs" sticking out of them. Thin Olde World Bronze and wash a side-load float in the shade areas on some of the berries and leaves to brighten them.

7 Finishing

Using a 1-inch (25mm) wash brush, apply three coats of J.W. etc. Right-Step Matte Varnish to finish the candle coaster. Add a cream candle to the holder and replace the glass globe. I hope these beautiful white poinsettias will light up your holidays!

Morning *Glories*
on a Table

In the Victorian language of flowers, the morning glory is a symbol of affection. These trumpet-shaped flowers are available in a delightful array of colors, including blue, white, red, rose-lavender, and white with blue stripes. In this lesson you will learn to **paint flowers that are made up of two shapes: a sphere and a cone.** Value and blending direction are important when creating the form of these flowers. The surface I chose is a small, round tea table, made to look like an antique.

Color Mixes

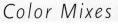

Mix 1
2 parts Wisteria + 1 part Light Buttermilk

Mix 2
1 part Wisteria + 1 part Deep Periwinkle

Mix 3
3 parts Deep Periwinkle + 1 part Wisteria

Mix 4
3 parts Soft Sage + 1 part Midnite Green

Mix 5
2 parts Admiral Blue + 1 part Deep Periwinkle

Mix 6
1 part Midnite Green + 1 part Soft Sage

Mix 7
1 part Mix 3 + 2 parts Deep Periwinkle

Mix 8
1 part Mix 4 + 2 parts Soft Sage

Mix 9
2 parts Light Buttermilk + 1 part Soft Sage

Mix 10
3 parts Midnite Green + 1 part Plantation Pine

Mix 11
2 parts Light Buttermilk + 1 part Wisteria

This pattern may be hand-traced or photocopied for personal use only. Enlarge at 213% on a photocopier to return to full size.

Materials

Surface

- This 22-inch (55.9cm) tall, 16-inch (40.6cm) diameter tea table is available from the Unfinished Furniture Mart, 1820 Pacific Coast Highway, Lomita, CA 90717. Phone: (310) 539-3631. Fax: (310) 539-4895.

DecoArt Americana Acrylic Paints

- Admiral Blue DA213
- Black Plum DA172
- Deep Periwinkle DA212
- Jade Green DA57
- Light Avocado DA106
- Light Buttermilk DA164
- Midnite Green DA84
- Plantation Pine DA113
- Royal Purple DA150
- Soft Sage DA207
- Titanium White DA1
- True Ochre DA143
- Wisteria DA211

DecoArt Heavenly Hues

- Heavenly Gold DHH17

Delta Ceramcoat Acrylic Paint

- Light Ivory 02401

Brushes

- ¼-inch (6mm), ⅜-inch (10mm), ½-inch (12mm) and ⅝-inch (15mm) angle brushes
- no. 10/0 script liner
- no. 1 round
- 1-inch (25mm) polyfoam brush
- 1-inch (25mm) wash brush

Additional Supplies

- Delta Ceramcoat Brown Antiquing Gel
- Liquitex Light Oak Gel Stain
- tracing paper
- black transfer paper
- wet palette
- 4" × 4" (10.2cm × 10.2cm) soft rags
- 320-grit wet/dry sandpaper
- tack rag
- 4-ounce (120ml) containers
- J.W. etc. White Lightning
- J.W. etc. Right-Step Matte Varnish

1 **Preparing the Surface**

Apply Light Oak Gel Stain to all parts of the table using a soft rag. Complete one part of the table before proceeding to the next area.

2 In a 4-ounce (120ml) container, mix 2 parts J.W. etc. White Lightning + 1 part Light Ivory. Using a polyfoam brush, apply two coats of this mix over all of the stained areas, allowing the first coat to dry before applying the second. When thoroughly dry, use 320-grit sandpaper to sand off some of the mixture you just applied. The more pressure you apply to the sandpaper, the more white paint will be removed, allowing the stain to show through. This will give the table an aged or distressed appearance. Wipe with a tack rag.

3 Pick up Brown Antiquing Gel on a soft rag and apply it to the outer edges of the table. Begin to rub the color in toward the center of the table. Also antique the spindle legs, lower shelf and feet, starting from the outside edges and rubbing into the larger areas. If the antiquing looks darker than desired, dampen a soft rag with clean water and wipe the areas that are too dark. When dry, repeat the antiquing process with Heavenly Gold. This color may seem to disappear into the antiquing, but it will enhance the wood without necessarily changing it. Use black transfer paper to transfer on all design lines.

4 Basecoating the Morning Glories and Leaves

Using a fully loaded ⅝-inch (15mm) angle brush or a brush that fits the area, base in the morning glories with the appropriate color listed below.

- Base morning glories A and C with Mix 2.
- Base morning glory B with Mix 1.
- Base morning glory D with Mix 3.
- Base the buds marked E with Mix 3.
- Base the buds marked F with Wisteria.

The morning glories may require more than one coat to achieve opaque coverage. Using a fully loaded ½-inch (12mm) angle brush, block in the leaves marked 1 with Jade Green, the leaves marked 2 with Soft Sage and the leaves marked 3 with

Mix 4. Pull in all vines, calyx and stems with a liner brush fully loaded with Jade Green.

Shade under the flip.

5 Applying Shade Values to the Leaves, Morning Glories and Buds

Using a ½-inch (12mm) angle brush, side-load float a shade of Light Avocado on all leaves marked 1. Shade leaves marked 2 with Jade Green and leaves marked 3 with Mix 6. Follow the arrows for stroke direction. Place the long side of the angle brush on the side where the arrows are. Apply full pressure in the wide areas of the leaves and release pressure as the area gets tighter. Allow the shading color to dry, then repeat for stronger coverage. Using a ⅝-inch (15mm) angle brush, side-load float the appropriate color listed at right on the morning glories. Side-load float the shading in front of the throat first, allowing the color to fade out in the direction of the arrows. Lay the long edge of the brush against the outside line of the flower and side-load float the color as you pull the brush

around the outer edge. The color should fade in toward the throat of the flower. After floating a section, use a mop brush or the dry chisel edge of the brush to sweep the color in the direction of the arrows. The colors can be repeated if stronger coverage is desired. Side-load float the buds across the tip and chisel the color toward the calyx.

- *Shade the morning glories marked A and C with Mix 5.*
- *Shade morning glory B with Mix 2.*
- *Shade morning glory D with Mix 7.*
- *Shade the buds marked E with Mix 7.*
- *Shade the buds marked F with Royal Purple.*

6 Applying Light Values to the Morning Glories, Leaves and Buds

Using a ½-inch (12mm) angle brush, side-load float a light value on the leaves marked 1 with Soft Sage, on leaves marked 2 with Mix 9 and on leaves marked 3 with Mix 8. Using a ½-inch (12mm) angle brush, side-load float the appropriate light value listed below and at right for the morning glories and buds. Side-load float inside the throat first and then in the center of the rolled area with a back-to-back float. Lighten the trumpeted areas by floating the color above the calyx or under the trumpet area. The arrows indicate the stroke direction. The light value areas are marked with Xs. Allow the first application of color to dry, then reapply.

- *Lighten morning glories A and C with Mix 1.*
- *Lighten morning glory B with Light Buttermilk.*

- *Lighten morning glory D with Mix 1.*
- *Lighten the buds marked E with Mix 1.*
- *Lighten the buds marked F with Light Buttermilk.*

Using a fully loaded no. 1 round, pull in the five raised lines on each open flower with the light mixture listed above and at left.

7 Building the Light and Dark Values on the Morning Glories, Leaves and Buds

In this step, continue to build darks and lights with side-load floats. Drybrushing can be used when applying the light values. Choose a brush that fits each area. When applying the colors, stay within the last application of color each time another color is applied. It's helpful to use a smaller brush or load less color across the brush as the areas of application get tighter. Using a 10/0 liner loaded with Soft Sage thinned with water, line in the vein lines on leaves 1 and 2. Use thinned Light Avocado and a 10/0 liner to line in the veins on the leaves marked 3. Using an angle brush that fits the area, side-load float the appropriate color listed at right to deepen the shading on the leaves.

- *Deepen leaves marked 1 with Plantation Pine, then Midnite Green.*
- *Deepen leaves marked 2 with Mix 10, then Midnite Green.*
- *Deepen leaves marked 3 with Light Avocado, then a touch of Plantation Pine (optional).*

The light values can be floated or drybrushed on the leaves using the appropriate color listed below.

- *Lighten leaves marked 1 with Light Buttermilk.*
- *Lighten leaves marked 2 with Soft Sage.*
- *Lighten leaves marked 3 with Light Buttermilk.*

Side-load float or drybrush the light values on the morning glories, using an angle brush that fits the area and the appropriate color listed below.

- *Lighten morning glories A and C with Wisteria, then Mix 11.*
- *Lighten morning glory B with Light Buttermilk, then Titanium White.*
- *Lighten morning glory D with Wisteria, then Mix 11.*
- *Lighten buds marked E and F with Mix 1.*

Using an angle brush that fits the area, side-load float the appropriate color listed below and at right to deepen the shade areas on the morning glories and buds.

- *Deepen morning glories A and C with Admiral Blue. Repeat for a deeper value.*
- *Deepen morning glory B with Deep Periwinkle. Repeat with Deep Periwinkle + a touch of Royal Purple.*
- *Deepen morning glory D with Deep Periwinkle. Repeat with Mix 5.*
- *Deepen the buds marked E with Deep Periwinkle.*
- *Deepen the buds marked F with Royal Purple.*

8 The Center Stamens

Using a no. 1 round, press three sit-down dots of Light Avocado in the centers of the open morning glories. When dry, press a smaller Soft Sage dot on the top of each of the previous dots. Place Black Plum at the bottom of each dot.

accent

Jade Green wash

tint

Jade Green wash

tint

Jade Green wash

accent

accent

9 Adding Final Darks, Highlights, Tints, Accents and Details

Using a ½-inch (12mm) angle brush, side-load float Black Plum accents on the tips or in the shade areas of the leaves. If a tint is desired on some of the leaves, use Royal Purple lightened with Wisteria. The leaves marked 1 may need to be warmed up with a very thin wash of True Ochre. Wash a very thin layer of Jade Green inside the throat of all of the open morning glories. Apply the accent color to the morning glories where marked using a thin side-load wash of Royal Purple. A stronger highlight can be applied by side-load floating or dry-brushing Light Buttermilk or Titanium White on the three morning glories that are grouped together. Repeat the final dark you applied if more dark is desired on any of the morning glories. Lighten the stems with Soft Sage. Drag thinned Soft Sage over the light areas. Using a small angle brush, side-load

float across the stems with Mix 10 to shade them. Repeat in some areas with a thin side-load float of Black Plum. Lighten the calyx leaves at the tip with Soft Sage and shade at the base with two side-load floats of Light Avocado. Deepen the shade with Mix 10. Place the strokes in on either end of the design using Light Avocado lightened with Jade Green and a liner brush. Using a 1-inch (25mm) wash brush, apply two to three coats of J.W. etc. Right-Step Matte Varnish to the table top, bottom shelf and legs, allowing each coat to dry before applying the next. The table is now ready to grace the room of your choice. It would make a lovely bedside table for your guest room—you might even want to paint a second one for the other side of the bed.

A Bouquet of *Flowers*
For You

In this lesson you will learn to combine several of the flowers from the past projects to create a bouquet. *In the previous lessons we have learned how to create form, how to use blending techniques, and how to develop a design using color relationship, value and background. Those skills will be repeated in this lesson with the emphasis on combining different flowers and leaves and creating a harmonious design.*

Color Mixes

Mix 1
1 part Titanium White +
1 part Eggshell

Mix 2
7 parts Titanium White +
1 part Moon Yellow

Mix 3
2 parts Titanium White +
1 part Mix 2

Mix 4
3 parts Mix 2 +
1 part Cranberry Wine

Mix 5
1 part Mix 4 +
1 part Cranberry Wine

Mix 6
3 parts Cranberry Wine
+ 1 part Ultra Blue Deep

Mix 7
3 parts Mix 3 +
1 part Mix 6

Mix 8
1 part Mix 3 +
1 part Mix 7

Mix 9
1 part Royal Purple
+ 1 part Mix 3

Mix 10
1 part Mix 9
+ 1 part Mix 3

Mix 11
Add a touch of Lamp
Black to some of Mix 6

Mix 12
1 part Mix 11 +
3 parts Mix 3

Mix 13
1 part Mix 11 +
1 part Mix 3

Mix 14
2 parts Cranberry Wine
+ 1 part Ultra Blue Deep

Mix 15
1 part Mix 14 +
3 parts Mix 2

Mix 16
1 part Mix 14 +
3 parts Mix 2

Mix 17
1 part Mix 16 +
2 parts Mix 3

Mix 18
1 part Mix 16
+ 2 parts Mix 3

Mix 19
Add a touch of Lamp
Black to some of Mix 11

Mix 20
1 part Olive Green
+ 2 parts Mix 3

Surface

This oval Masonite panel with 19" × 11" (48.3cm × 27.9cm) frame (item no. 118A) is available from Bush's Smoky Mountain Wood Products, 3556 Wilhite Road, Sevierville, TN 37876-6602. Phone: (865) 453-4828.

DecoArt Americana Acrylic Paints
- Black Plum DA172
- Cranberry Wine DA112
- Eggshell DA153
- Jade Green DA57
- Lamp Black DA67
- Light Avocado DA106
- Marigold DA194
- Midnite Green DA84
- Moon Yellow DA7
- Olive Green DA56
- Plantation Pine DA113
- Royal Purple DA150
- Taupe DA109
- Titanium White DA1
- Ultra Blue Deep DA100

Delta Ceramcoat Acrylic Paint
- Gleams 14K Gold 02604

Brushes
- ⅛-inch (3mm), ¼-inch (6mm), ⅜-inch (10mm), ½-inch (12mm), ⅝-inch (15mm) and ¾-inch (19mm) angle brushes
- no. 10/0 script liner
- no. 6 round
- 1-inch (25mm) polyfoam brush
- 1-inch (25mm) wash brush

Additional Supplies
- tracing paper
- black and white transfer papers
- Sta-Wet palette
- waxed palette pad
- Designs From the Heart Wood Sealer
- 320-grit wet/dry sandpaper
- tack rag
- J.W. etc. Right-Step Matte Varnish

1 Setting the Theme and Choosing the Surface

For this piece I knew I wanted to create a soft, Victorian arrangement that could be placed in a formal setting but still have a springtime appearance.

The surface I chose was an oval Masonite panel in a rectangular frame that had elements of the oval shape repeated on the top and bottom. The surface is simple but has elegant lines that could be repeated in the flowers and leaves; this will enhance and support the design, not detract from it.

2 Choosing the Flowers

Choosing the flowers that would be used in the composition was the next step. I looked through my previous designs for flowers that would work best with the theme and surface I'd chosen.

First I needed a flower for the center of interest. This flower needed to be the largest, having interest and shape and design lines that would complement the background surface. I decided the iris is the one that could stand alone because it is larger then the others, it has multiple petals, and the long and narrow shape of the petals fits the background shape. I placed the iris in the upper center of the surface.

Next I needed flowers to support the iris. These needed to add more interest to the center area while also leading the eye away from the center. Pansies repeated the number of petals in the iris and their shape provided continuity. Tulips are a springtime flower that complemented the theme, while adding height and length, following the length of the oval background.

Finally, I chose roses as filler flowers to complete the arrangement and keep with the Victorian theme. Showing only a

portion of the roses changed their round shape to an oval, which relates to the tulips, and the oval shape of the surface.

3 Adding the Leaves

Leaves will support and add interest to complete the arrangement. When choosing flowers it is important that the shape of their leaves will complement the design, not distract from it. The shapes of the leaves in this design are all very similar—the iris and tulip have cylindrical leaves while the rose and pansy leaves are rectangular—providing continuity and support.

4 Adding Filler Flowers

At this point I decided that the arrangement needed a second filler flower that would anchor the design to the background while softening the hard design lines. For this baby's breath or lilacs could be used.

5 Creating a Composition

To create your composition, you could select elements from other designs or from photographs and trace the basic shapes onto tracing paper. Cut each element out and then move the elements around like pieces of a puzzle until you achieve a pleasing composition.

Or you could simply draw the basic shapes of the elements freehand, using other designs or photos as a reference.

6 Sketch in the Basic Flower Shapes

Once you have selected the elements of the design, draw the basic shapes of the flowers onto paper using a pencil. Start in the center of interest area. If the overall design needs to be altered, erase and insert another basic shape.

7 Refining the Basic Shapes

Starting in the center of interest area, begin to refine and draw shapes within the basic lines of the petals and leaves. Work on the outside line areas, developing the shapes of all the elements of the design.

XXX can be used to indicate light areas.

8 *Determining the Lights and Darks*

Once you've completed the form of each element, chose the direction of the light source. The light direction for this design is coming straight on, slightly to the right. The shadows will fall opposite the light areas. Using the side of the pencil, begin to add shading within each petal and leaf, creating more form and dimension in the design. This light direction will cast shadows behind each flower and leaf; this will bring some objects close and push some objects to the back. The back-ground, or negative space, will also need to be shaded as the entire design will cast a shadow onto the background. To help you see shadows it is helpful to place small Xs where the light may strike each petal and each area of the leaves. The light hits in the lightest area and begins to fade into a shadow. The smallest or tightest areas where no light can reach are the darkest shadows.

The labels on the image read:
Tulip 2
Tulip 3
Tulip 1
Rose 2
Rose 1
Pansy 1
Pansy 3
Pansy 2
Rose 5
Rose 4
Rose 3

9 The design is complete. Trace a final pattern using pen and ink. The pattern is ready to be transferred onto the surface.

10 Choosing a Color Scheme

I chose an analogous color scheme for this design—red-violet, violet, blue-violet, red and red-orange—with red-violet as the dominate color. The addition of the complement yellow-green is needed for the leaves. I used a cool, neutral white for the background color.

To create a soft, pastel painting, I used grayed-down versions of all of the colors rather than using them in their purest forms.

Next, I assigned a color to each flower based on its relation to the center of interest area. The lightest, brightest and warmest colors should be placed in the center of interest area.

11 Preparing the Surface

Seal the frame with Designs From the Heart Wood Sealer. When dry, sand the frame with 320-grit sandpaper and then apply two coats of Eggshell. Basecoat the Masonite panel with three coats of Mix 1, allowing to dry and sanding between each coat. Transfer the design lines to the panel using black transfer paper. Wash over the frame with a thin wash of Mix 1. Paint the routed edge on the inside and outside of the frame with 14K Gold; a second coat may be needed for solid coverage. Next, thin 14K Gold with water and spatter lightly on the frame and the oval edges of the panel.

12 Basing in the Design

Please refer to the previous projects for instructions on painting the individual flowers and leaves, substituting the colors on these pages. Refer to the drawings and the picture on page 125 to add in the placement of the color values. Thin the paint to a wash and apply several coats to achieve solid coverage.

- Base in the iris with Mix 8.
- Base pansy 1 with Mix 10 on the front three petals and Mix 9 on the back two petals.
- Base pansy 2 with Mix 13.
- Base pansy 3 with Mix 16.
- Base tulip 1 with Mix 13.
- Base tulip 2 with Mix 18.
- Base tulip 3 with Mix 8.
- Base roses 1 and 2 with Mix 4.
- Base roses 3, 4 and 5 with Mix 18.
- Base all leaves with Jade Green.

13 Apply Color to the Area Behind the Design

Refer to the instructions in project 4 for this technique, substituting the following colors: Float behind the design with Eggshell, then apply thin floats of Jade Green here and there. Apply Taupe where the filler flowers will be placed. When dry, deepen the areas with thin floats of Mix 17 and Black Plum.

14 Building Light and Dark Values on the Flowers

Using a side load of Taupe, begin to place in the flower petals. When dry, wash over the petals with very thin Royal Purple or Black Plum. Build lighter petals using Mix 18. Dots can be placed in the center of a few flowers using Mix 20. The colors for each flower are listed in the order they will be used; if further information is needed, refer to the instructions in previous projects.

Iris
- Paint the first shade with Mix 7.
- Paint the first light with a brush mix of Mix 8 + Mix 3.
- Paint the second light with Mix 3.
- Paint the second shade with Mix 8.
- Paint the darks with Mix 8.
- Paint the highlights with a brush mix of Mix 3 + Titanium White.
- Paint the tints with thinned Cranberry Wine or Royal Purple.

Pansy 1
- Paint the first shade with Mix 9; use Royal Purple for the back petals.
- Paint the first light with Mix 10 lightened with Mix 2; use Mix 10 on the back petals.
- Create the second shade by applying Mix 9 again; reapply Royal Purple for the back petals.
- Paint the second light by adding Mix 3 to the first light; use Mix 10 lightened with Mix 2 for the back petals.
- Apply the darks with Royal Purple on the front petals; add a touch of Lamp Black to Royal Purple for the back petals.
- Add a Mix 3 highlight to the front petals if needed.

Pansy 2
- Paint the first shade with Mix 12.
- Paint the first light with Mix 2 added to Mix 13.
- Darken Mix 12 with Mix 11 for the second shade.
- Add more Mix 2 to the first light for the second light.
- Use Mix 11 for the darks.
- Highlight with Mix 2.

Pansy 3
- Paint the first shade with Mix 15.
- Add Mix 2 to Mix 16 for the first light.
- Darken Mix 15 with Mix 14 for the second shade.
- For the second light add more Mix 2 to the first light.

- Use Mix 14 for the darks.
- Highlight with Mix 2.

Roses 1 and 2

- Shade using Mix 5. When dry, deepen the shade using Cranberry Wine.
- Overstroke using a brush double loaded with Mix 4 on one side and Mix 3 on the other. When dry, lighten the overstrokes with Mix 3.
- Use thin floats of Black Plum for the darks.

Roses 3, 4 and 5

- Shade with a float of Mix 17.
- Overstroke with a double load of Mix 18 on one side and Mix 3 on the other side of the brush.
- Highlight the strokes using Mix 3 + Titanium White.
- Apply thin floats of Black Plum to reinforce the shade areas.

Tulip 1

- Paint the first shade with Mix 12.
- Paint the first light with Mix 2 added to Mix 13.
- Darken Mix 12 with Mix 18 for the second shade.
- Add more Mix 2 to the first light for the second light.
- Paint the darks with Mix 18.
- Highlight with Mix 2.

Tulip 2

- Paint the first shade with Mix 17.
- Add Mix 2 to Mix 18 for the first light.
- Darken Mix 17 with a touch of Cranberry Wine for the second shade.
- Add more Mix 2 to the first light for the second light.
- Paint the darks with Cranberry Wine cooled with a touch of Black Plum.
- Highlight with Mix 2.
- Float a tint on the upper right side with Mix 16.

Tulip 3

- Paint the first shade with Mix 7.
- Add Mix 2 to Mix 8 for the first light.
- Darken Mix 7 with Mix 19 for the second shade.
- Add more Mix 2 to the first light for the second light.
- Add more Mix 19 to the second shade for the darks.
- Highlight with Mix 2.
- Tint the left side of the vein lines with thinned Mix 17.

15 Applying Light and Dark Values to the Leaves

The colors are listed at right in the order they are used. If further information is needed, refer to the leaf instructions given on pages 18-21.

Tulip and Iris Leaves

- Add Mix 20 to Jade Green for the first light.
- Paint the first shade with Light Avocado.
- Add more Mix 20 for the second light.
- Reapply Light Avocado for the second shade.
- Use Mix 14 for the darks.
- Highlight with Mix 3.
- Accent with Cranberry Wine.

Rose and Pansy Leaves

- Paint the first shade with Jade Green + Light Avocado.
- Paint the first light with Eggshell.
- Paint the second shade with Light Avocado.
- Add Mix 3 to the first light for the second light.
- Paint the darks with Plantation Pine.
- Paint the very dark areas with Midnite Green.
- Highlight with Mix 3.
- Accent with Cranberry Wine, Mix 14, Black Plum or Royal Purple.
- Tint with Mix 5, Mix 10 or Mix 18.
- Line the veins on the leaves with the second light value.

16 Finish the Flower Centers and Detail Linework

Pansies

Using a liner brush loaded with Mix 18, line in the pansy beards on all three flowers. Still using the liner, place small lines of Moon Yellow into the beards. When dry, float a shade of Marigold. Place a press dot of Cranberry Wine in the triangle space. Using Titanium White, pull in comma strokes on both sides of the triangle space.

Roses

Using a liner, place dots in the center using Marigold toned down with a touch of Black Plum. When dry, add a few Moon Yellow dots, then a few with Mix 2.

Iris

Using a liner, tap in Marigold toned down with a touch of Black Plum. When dry, tap in Moon Yellow, then Mix 2.

17 *Finishing*

Using a 1-inch (25mm) wash brush, apply two or three coats of J.W. etc. Right-Step Matte Varnish to the panel and frame. Creating your own bouquet can be fun; why not try putting together your own flowers? The possibilities are endless.

Resources

Allen Wood Crafts

3020 Dogwood Lane, Rt. 3
Supulpa, OK 74066
Phone: (918) 224-8796
Fax: (919) 224-3208
(Project 7 slant-top box)

Barb Watson Brushworks

P.O. Box 1467
Moreno Valley, CA 92556
Phone: (909) 653-3780
Web site: www.barbwatson.com
(Project 2 metal bowl)

Binney & Smith

Phone: (888) 422-7954
Web site: www.liquitex.com
(Liquitex Light Oak Gel Stain)

Brenda Stewart by Design

228 Yorkshire Dr.
Williamsburg, VA 21385
Phone: (757) 564-7093
(Project 5 porcelain plate)

Bush's Smoky Mountain Wood Products

3556 Wilhite Rd.
Sevierville, TN 37876-6602
Phone: (865) 453-4828
(Project 10 oval with frame)

Chroma, Inc.

205 Bucky Dr.
Lititz, PA 17543
Phone: (800) 257-8278
E-mail: info@chroma-inc.com
Web site:
http://www.chroma-inc.com/josonja/
(Jo Sonja All Purpose Sealer)

Cutting Edge, The

343 Twin Pines Dr.
Glendale, OR 97442
Phone: (909) 464-0440
(Project 4 stationery box)

DecoArt

P.O. Box 327
Stanford, KY 40484
Phone: (606) 365-3193
Fax: (606) 365-9739
E-mail: paint@decoart.com
Web site: www.decoart.com
(Americana and Heavenly Hues
acrylic paints and products)

Delta Technical Coatings, Inc.,

2550 Pellissier Place
Whittier, CA 90601
Phone: (800) 423-4135
Fax: (562) 695-5157
Web site: www.deltacrafts.com
(Ceramcoat acrylic paints)

Designs From the Heart

4568 Ellery Dr.
Columbus, OH 43227
Phone: (740) 548-7469
(Wood sealer)

Golden Artist Colors, Inc.

188 Bell Rd.
New Berlin, NY 13411-9527
Phone: (607) 847-6154
Fax: (607) 847-6767
E-mail: goldenart@goldenpaints.com
Web site: www.goldenpaints.com
(Golden acrylic paints)

Hofcraft

P.O. Box 72-W
Grand Haven, MI 49417
Phone: (616) 847-8822
E-mail: hofcraft@hofcraft.com
Web site: www.hofcraft.com
(Project 3 single pie carrier basket)

J.W. etc.

2205 First St., Suite 103
Simi Valley, CA 93065
Phone: (805) 526-5066

Fax: (805) 526-1297
E-mail: jwetc@earthlink.net
Web site: www.jwetc.com
(White Lightning, Right-Step
Matte Varnish)

Krylon

Phone: (800) 4 KRYLON
Web site: www.krylon.com
(Krylon Matte Finish Spray, no.
1311)

Plaid Enterprises, Inc.

Attn: Customer Service
3225 Westech Drive
Norcross, GA 30092
Phone: (800) 842-4197
E-mail: talk@plaidonline.com
Web site: www.plaidonline.com
(Decorator Glaze, Simply Stencils
Scrolling Vine, no. 28172)

Pop Shop, The

Norman & Simone Guillemette
RR 2 Box 1524
New Dam Rd.
Sanford, ME 04073
Phone: (207) 324-5946
Web site:
www.cybertours.com/~popshop/
pophome.htm
(Project 6 basket)

Royal & Langnickel Brush Mfg.

6707 Broadway
Merrillville, IN 46410
(Langnickel brushes)

Stonebridge Collection

4411 Bee Ridge Rd., Suite 256
Sarasota, FL 34233
Phone: (800) ART TOLE
(Project 8 candle/wine coaster)

Unfinished Furniture Mart
   1820 Pacific Coast Highway
   Lomita, CA 90717
   Phone: (310) 539-3631
   Fax: (310) 539-4895
   (Project 9 tea table)

Viking Woodcrafts, Inc.
   1317 8th St. SE
   Waseca, MN 56093
   Phone: (800) 361-0115
   Fax: (507) 835-3895
   Web site: www.vikingwoodcrafts.com
   (Project 1 towel holder)

The following Canadian retailers may also carry the supplies used in this book:

Crafts Canada
   2745 29th St. NE
   Calgary, ON
   T1Y 7B5

Folk Art Enterprises
   PO Box 1088
   Ridgetown, ON
   N0P 2C0
   Phone: (888) 214-0062

MacPherson Craft Wholesale
   83 Queen St. E.
   PO Box 1870
   St. Mary's, ON
   N4X 1C2
   Phone: (519) 284-1741

Maureen McNaughton Enterprises
   RR #2
   Bellwood, ON
   N0B 1J0
   Phone: (519) 843-5648

Mercury Art & Craft Supershop
   332 Wellington St.
   London, ON
   N6C 4P7
   Phone: (519) 434-1636

Town & Country Folk Art Supplies
   93 Green Lane
   Thornhill, ON
   L3T 6K6
   Phone: (905) 882-0199

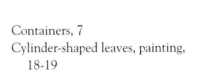

Index